THE RETIREE'S GUIDE TO HOUSING WEALTH

5 Ways the New Reverse Mortgage Is Changing Retirement

DON GRAVES, RICP®, CLTC®, CSA

Foreword by Ed Slott, CPA

ISBN: 978-1-7320270-2-2

DISCLAIMER

The examples and case studies in the book are given for
illustrative purposes only. They should not be considered tax,
financial planning, or legal advice. Individuals should consult a
professional with regards to their specific situation.

Moreover, any calculations illustrated are reflective of the
program rates and terms at the time of publication.

TABLE OF CONTENTS

ED SLOTT FOREWORD

I used to be one of those people who said, "Stay away from reverse mortgages!" Then I saw that the reverse mortgage topic seemed to be growing in popularity in the advisor community. As an educator, it's very important to me to know if my ideas are still correct, so I gathered together articles and several books and did some research.

In my exploration, one book stood out in particular. It's actually the book you're holding in your hands written by Don Graves, retirement specialist and reverse mortgage expert. From his 20+ years of experience communicated in the following pages, I found out I was basing my ideas on old stories and outdated fears about reverse mortgages.

By the time I finished reading, my concerns had been addressed and a new world of retirement strategies had been opened. I asked myself, "Why didn't anyone present this information so clearly before?" That is Don's gift. He explained the reverse mortgage program in a way that was easy to understand, and it made me wonder: how many more people aren't being informed about how the "new" reverse mortgage works and how it can provide additional funds for retirement?

Why is this important? Over the last 30 years and from the feedback I've received from advisors and the millions of people who have watched my PBS specials, I've discovered that today's retirement has many concerns, but one stands out more than the others: longevity. Whether for better or worse people are living longer and they're worried about their money lasting.

As a result, many retirees are lacking financial security and peace of mind from a retirement plan, and it may be because they haven't considered all their retirement assets. They're not using all the cards they have to play, so to speak.

One of those cards is their home equity. For many retirees, equity is tied up in their home and not being put to use. This is where the reverse mortgage can help, by giving you access to your equity for use in retirement planning.

For me as a tax advisor, one of the most important planning aspects of the program is that the funds are tax-free. If you've ever seen my PBS special or read my books, you know that having tax-free sources of income in retirement is very important. To me, taxes are the single biggest factor that separates people from their retirement dreams.

Having more tax-free income isn't for splurging and spending. It's for peace of mind. You want to know: will my money last as long as I do? The reverse mortgage is another tool in the toolkit to help give you financial security for the rest of your life.

I'm not saying the reverse mortgage is for everyone, but it has changed and it's to your benefit to consider all of your assets. In fact, I have included information about this book in my PBS program materials because I wanted the audience to be exposed to the new, updated and accurate information found in it. I recommend you read it. Ultimately, it's about educating yourself and learning the questions to ask when considering this strategy.

Ed Slott, CPA
Retirement Expert | Founder of www.irahelp.com

INTRODUCTION

The book you're reading is based on more than 14,000 personal conversations over the last 20 years with retirees, their families, and financial advisors. In that time, I've encountered retirement plans that were right on track and more than a few that were not. I've heard retirees' concerns and suspicions about reverse mortgages and have seen their relief when they discover the truth for themselves.

Before we begin our journey together, I want to share three things you can expect:

Common Sense Clarity

The purpose of this book is to provide an overview of how the newly restructured reverse mortgage fits into retirement planning. I've distilled more than two decades of real-life encounters into practical, back-of-the-napkin, common sense strategies. The goal is not an academic deep dive (though, we have an entire section on advanced strategies), but a basic primer—simplicity without being simplistic.

Case Studies and Conversations

You will find real stories from my past clients, including their challenges, and I'll outline the steps and conversations that led them to their informed decision. The scenarios will vary, but undoubtedly, you will find your situation represented. When you do, pay close attention to how the pros and cons of the reverse mortgage are weighed.

Commitment to the Advisor's Role

You will also find accounts of people seeking advice from their advisors. Some of these advisors are their peers, others are realtors or accountants, but the majority are financial advisors. This is emphasized because, for most people, the presence of a skilled, retirement-income-focused advisor can provide superior outcomes and help them sleep better at night.

That said, even financial advisors vary from firm to firm. Some have an education/information-only focus with reverse mortgages. Others will be able to explain some of its broader concepts and key strategical uses. Regardless of the type of advisor you engage, be sure they have a cursory knowledge of how reverse mortgages work. I wrote an entire book just for advisors - Housing Wealth: 3 Ways the New Reverse Mortgage Is Changing Retirement Income Conversations [An Advisor's Guide]

Over the course of their history, reverse mortgages have proven to be a great tool for thousands of retirees, but they're not always the right option. So, I will make a bold promise. If you read this book with an open mind, I guarantee that by the time you finish, you will have a better, deeper, richer understanding of what the reverse mortgage is, how it works, when it's appropriate and when it's not. And, most importantly, if it is the right tool for your retirement.

SECTION 1:

THE CHANGING RETIREMENT INCOME LANDSCAPE

Ten Questions to Get Started

Retirement has changed significantly from what our grandparents and even our parents experienced not too long ago. We're living longer, healthier lives, but with that comes the added stress of maintaining your desired lifestyle for a lengthier retirement.

You know it's necessary to plan ahead and consider all your available retirement tools, but is it possible you're overlooking the most valuable tool of all – your Housing Wealth?

I've invested my time and energy over the past 20 years to help people just like you understand the importance of their Housing Wealth, how to best access it, and how to use it efficiently in their retirements.

To begin, I always ask my clients and their families this question: Are you making full use of your Housing Wealth to create the type of retirement you most desire?

In order to truly determine the answer, I've developed an easy, 10-question assessment for you to take. The assessment will do the hard work for you. It determines if the new reverse mortgage could work for your particular situation. Although it does not explore every question that could be asked, it does provide enough insight to determine if continuing the journey makes sense.

Whether for yourself or on behalf of a friend or family member, I ask you to take three minutes and honestly answer the questions. You will have the choice of selecting Yes, No or Not Sure/Not Applicable. Let's get started!

Question	Yes	No	Not Sure/Applicable
Am I, or my spouse age 62, or older, and own a home?			
Am I planning to stay in my home for at least the next 5 years?			

Question	Yes	No	Not Sure/ Applicable
Do I currently have a monthly loan payment?			
Would eliminating a mandatory monthly loan payment be helpful?			
Am I open to moving if it meant a better retirement lifestyle and added savings?			
Would having access to additional monthly income, if needed, be helpful?			
Do I have any concerns that my savings will last for the duration of my retirement?			
Is it important to me to have a back-up plan for stock market volatility and inflation?			
Would it be valuable to have a tax-free reserve fund to cover unexpected expenses, emergencies or unplanned purchases?			
If my out-of-pocket healthcare costs exceeded $100,000, would this be a strain on my retirement savings?			

Understanding Your Score

Simply add up how many times you answered Yes and follow the corresponding suggestion.

0-1 times

It looks like you don't need this book at present. Perhaps you know someone who would benefit from reading it; feel free to pass it on.

2-3 times

You may find only some sections of this book will be helpful; perhaps skip to Section Five: Additional and Advanced Strategies.

4-6 times

This book will absolutely offer you helpful advice; pay close attention to Section Three: The Five Foundations of Housing Wealth.

7 or more

You're exactly in the right position for this book to offer the most value; don't skip a single word.

2

Something Has Changed

A few years ago, I received a call from a retired CEO of a large multinational pharmaceutical company who was interested in a reverse mortgage. What was interesting is that he had a 5-million-dollar retirement portfolio and a 4.5-million dollar home.

More commonly, I receive this type of call - the family of an 85-year-old woman, who had gotten a reverse mortgage 15 years ago, contacts me because their mom's health is failing, her income is limited, and she needs extra money each month to cover home health aides. The family now wants to find out how to activate the "income convertibility" feature of the line of credit to fund the added expenses.

These phone calls tell us two things:

- The profile of today's reverse mortgage borrower is shifting.

- The program may offer retirement strategies you hadn't considered, or even knew existed.

Today's Reverse Mortgage Borrowers Look Different

For years, it was wrongly believed that reverse mortgages were just for house rich, cash poor seniors (though, they never really were). Today's savvy retirees are more sophisticated, well-read, and pro-active in doing their homework and are finding something different.

Here's a short description of the types of retirees we find considering housing wealth today.

 The Constrained: Those who are focused on financial survival. They have found themselves in dire circumstances with little to no savings/assets and limited monthly income.

The Concerned: Those who are focused on rescuing retirement income. Their retirement plan has encountered something unexpected. Perhaps one spouse had planned to work longer, but couldn't, or an unexpected health crisis drained their savings faster than expected.

The Cautious: Those who are focused on increasing contingency. They have a workable retirement plan, but not enough reserved for the unexpected or undesirable: prolonged poor markets, higher-than-expected inflation, unwise portfolio draws during bear markets, etc.

The Comfortable: Those who are focused on improving retirement plans. They have a workable (or nearly workable) retirement plan but desire enhancement: increased retirement spending, the creation of a hedge for market corrections, establishment of legacy gifting with asset protection, life insurance, etc.

The Carefree: These are the Bill Gates, Oprah Winfreys and Warren Buffets of the world. They are seemingly not going to run out of money - ever - yet, even some of them are exploring reverse mortgages for strategic purposes.

Thanks to the recent research of scholars, institutions, and financial thought leaders, this is a very different list of borrowers than just a few years ago. These changes also extend to the various ways the reverse mortgage is being used.

Today's Reverse Mortgage Strategies Do More

CAUTIOUS
Workable retirement plan, but needs improvement and contingency.

CONCERNED
Retirement plan needs a rescue.
Something unexpected happened.

COMFORTABLE
Workable retirement plan, but desire enhancement.

CONSTRAINED
Dire circumstances.
Fixed income.
Little to no other savings.

CAREFREE
Solid retirement plan with capacity to weather any shocks.

As an educator, I often speak with financial professionals. When I do, I always begin my presentation by asking them how many of their retired clients do they think would actually need a reverse mortgage. Their answer is usually between 5-10%.

Then I ask, if there were a proven resource that allowed their clients to:

- Increase Cash Flow
- Reduce Retirement Income Risks
- Preserve Assets
- Improve Liquidity (access to dollars when needed)
- Add New Dollars Back into Retirement Savings

What percentage of their clients would want to know about this? The answer, of course, is 100%.

That's what has changed. Initially, most people I meet don't think they (or their clients/family member) would ever benefit from a reverse mortgage. Then I explain what the newly restructured reverse mortgage is designed to do, and interest levels jump to 100%. An entirely new conversation is opened.

- **Increasing Cash Flow:** I can imagine you have an interest in learning how to have more accessible cash for your retirement enjoyment and expenses.

- **Reducing Risks:** Your retirement may be long and unpredictable. Would you like to have a safety net, backup plan, or "insurance policy" for the things that can go sideways?

- **Preserving Assets:** There are all types of eroding factors that can eat away at your retirement savings. Some are out of your control but not all. Having a proven resource for preservation could be a game-changer!

- **Improving Liquidity:** Life is filled with "what-ifs." Having readily accessible access to tax-free dollars when those "what-ifs" occur could bring you the peace of mind you desire.

- **Adding New Dollars to Savings:** Would you be interested in hearing about a way to add $50,000 - $250,000 back into your retirement savings? I imagine yes!

That's right! These five things are the core benefits of the newly restructured reverse mortgage.

Why the huge gap between the typical perception about the reverse mortgage and the reality of what one accomplishes? I have a theory. In 1997, I was president of Habitat for Humanity in Philadelphia. The board of directors provided me with my first cell phone. A cell phone! I'd hit the big time. However, the phone only did two things: made and received phone calls, period!

Fast-forward twenty years to my son's smartphone. I've seen many texts sent, Angry Birds die, videos published, Snapchats come and go, and Facebook opinions posted, but the one thing I rarely see my son do is make or receive a phone call!

See the disconnect? When some people think of the reverse mortgage, they envision the equivalent of my 1997 cell phone. It was useful and timely for the era but limited in scope when compared with modern resources.

However, today's newly restructured reverse mortgage is much more like my son's smartphone. It has a myriad of applications, or apps, that can help retirees create new and powerful retirement outcomes.

3

Preparing for a Longer and Less Predictable Retirement

R etirement has changed! It is going to last longer and be less predictable than ever before. If that isn't daunting enough, add the current economic and political climate, and it begins to get even more concerning.

In order to formulate a plan that will get you the retirement of your dreams, you must know what you're facing and be prepared for expected and even unexpected challenges.

The Rules Have Changed

Work longer, spend less, and save more are more often the rules for retirement than the exceptions. For many, seventy is the new sixty-two. Three overarching themes about today's retiree and pre-retiree are at the root of the problem.

- Retirees are living longer than previous generations. Instead of spanning fifteen or twenty years, today's retirement will last twenty-five, thirty, or even thirty-five years or more. This length of time is something most people have not planned for.

- Retirees have not saved enough to sustain retirement income for their projected lifespan. A longer retirement necessitates additional funding; add inflation and global economic uncertainty to the mix, and you've got one expensive quarter-century to plan for. Even an attempt to increase saving in the years leading up to retirement will not make up for the compounding interest that could have been earned over the course of their careers.

- Retirees will carry more consumer debt into retirement than previous generations. Much of the baby boomers' money in retirement will be tied up in debt they accumulated during their working years. This can be especially problematic when transitioning to fixed income.

The Risks Are Different

Traditionally, retirement planning was focused on getting to the top of the mountain, sometimes compared to climbing Mount Everest - a metaphor that leaves no illusions about retirement challenges.

The goal was to save all you could, get to the top, plant your flag, and live off what you had amassed. This is commonly referred to as the Accumulation Phase, and its primary focus is on asset allocation - diversifying holdings among different types of investments to balance risks and rewards.

But it's the second part of the retirement journey, the descent - also known as the Distribution or Decumulation phase - that has proved to be the more difficult of the two because financial risks don't dissipate upon entering retirement; they increase!

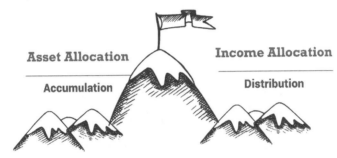

Asset Allocation   **Income Allocation**

Accumulation   **Distribution**

18 Risks in Retirement

1. Longevity Risk
2. Inflation Risk
3. Excessive Withdrawal Risk
4. Health Expense Risk
5. Long-Term Care Risk
6. Market Risk
7. Fragility Risk
8. Financial Elder Abuse Risk
9. Interest Rate Risk
10. Liquidity Risk
11. Sequence of Returns Risk
12. Forced Retirement Risk
13. Re-Employment Risk
14. Employer Insolvency Risk
15. Loss of Spouse Risk
16. Unexpected Financial Responsibility Risk
17. Timing Risk
18. Public Policy Risk

 You can find the complete list with definitions at www.18risks.com

Once you retire, there is a heightened risk of running out of savings or having to substantially reduce your lifestyle. The American College of Financial Services where I teach has identified eighteen major risks distinctly associated with and amplified by descending the retirement mountain.

Throughout the book, we will touch on a few of the bigger risks. Right now, I will briefly highlight four.

Longevity Risk The fate of living too long. We also consider this a risk multiplier because it escalates all the other retirement income risks.

Inflation Risk The inability of investments and savings to keep pace with inflation. Inflation simply means products and goods are more expensive over time. Obviously, this can have a devastating effect on retirement. When inflation rates are high, a retiree's savings don't go as far, and this can significantly impact the survival rate of the retiree's portfolio. As rates increase, more money must be pulled from the portfolio, eroding it more quickly.

Market Risk/Volatility It is well known that the value of your retirement accounts will go up and down based on market performance. When market dips occur while "climbing the mountain," most people can ride out the storm. However, when dips happen once savings are being spent, the consequences can be devastating. In the foundations section and advanced applications, we will talk more about risk, volatility, and the ways housing wealth can address them.

Healthcare Risk The "silent killer" of retirement income. Most retirees don't plan for the potential out-of-pocket healthcare costs that are associated with retirement. Modest projections put the value of these costs at more than $280,000 for the average retiring, married couple.

The rules have changed, and the dangers have grown. It's no longer enough to get to the top of the retirement mountain and plant your financial flag. You must understand the dangers of decumulation and have a plan to address the risks that will occur.

In the next chapter, we'll discern together what your specific challenges are by asking five questions.

4

The Five Biggest Retirement Questions Every Retiree Must Answer

> "If I had an hour to solve a problem and my life depended on the solution, I would spend the first 55 minutes determining the proper question to ask, for once I know the proper question, I could solve the problem in less than five minutes."
>
> - Albert Einstein

Effective questions about retirement should reveal two things: (1) what the specific problem is that you're facing and (2) how it is affecting your well-being and peace of mind. Putting in the work upfront to ask and answer the right retirement questions will place you that much closer to the worry-free retirement you deserve.

- **What is keeping you up at night?**
- **What brings you the most worry?**
- **In what area are you experiencing financial stress?**
- **How often do you think about money?**
- **Are you concerned for your spouse should you pass away?**
- **How often do you consider the "what-ifs" of retirement?**

Over the years, I've collected the most common answers to these questions and created five, overarching questions that represent the essential retirement concerns most retirees have (or should have). I've found them to be foundational and will base the housing wealth strategies on them. They all begin with the letter L.

The 5 L's

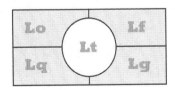

The Longevity Question

 Will I have enough savings to meet my basic living expenses?

According to most surveys, the number one concern of retirees continues to be "running out of savings." And for good reason, we are living longer, and longevity is one of the most dangerous retirement risks because it exacerbates and multiplies the impact of all the other risks.

A Historical Perspective on Life Expectancy

Declaration of Independence
July 1776
Life Expectancy
AGE 36

Civil War Ends
May 1865
Life Expectancy
AGE 42

Social Security Act
August 1935
Life Expectancy
AGE 62

Medicare Enacted
July 1965
Life Expectancy
AGE 68

Today
Life Expectancy
Approaching
AGE 80

Male Avg. Age
84.3

Social Security Administration

Female Avg. Age
86.6

A man reaching age 65 today can expect to live, on average, until age 84.3.

A woman turning age 65 today can expect to live, on average, until age 86.6.

For a couple who are presently age 65, there is a 50% chance that one person will live to see age 92.

How Does Longevity Impact Retirement Savings?

Most people don't think they are going to live as long as they actually will, and this miscalculation can lead to hundreds of thousands of dollars that you have not saved for.

Let's say a 65-year-old couple has a 1-million-dollar nest egg from which they are currently drawing $50,000 a year. By the time they turn age 85 (assuming a 3% inflation adjustment), they will be drawing closer to $90,000 a year. If one or more of them lives to age 90 (5 additional years), they will need an additional $500,000 in savings. If one lives to age 95 (10 additional years), they will need an extra 1-million dollars in savings, or to significantly change their lifestyle.

This example shows that in retirement planning, a primary focus must be on the lifetime survival of savings to meet essential living requirements: food, housing, medical expenses, etc.

With longevity in mind, here's the question you must answer:

On a scale of 1 to 10, how much does the thought of running out of savings in retirement trouble you? (Circle your number)

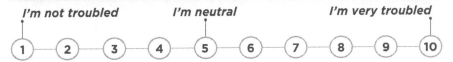

I'm not troubled   *I'm neutral*   *I'm very troubled*

1   2   3   4   5   6   7   8   9   10

The Lifestyle Question

Will I have enough money to enjoy retirement on my terms?

It's one thing to have enough savings to meet your basic needs, but it's another to maintain your desired overall standard of living. These lifestyle components tend to be more discretionary in nature and may include things like travel and leisure, self-improvement activities, social engagements, and helping a family member.

Typically, I see retirees choose one of two ways.

"It Will All Work Out in the End"

For many, spending desires exceed the allowable budget, and this is most clearly felt in the early phases of retirement. This dilemma causes retirees to make some very serious choices - roll the dice, spend more, and hope their investments perform better than expected, or that they may not live as long as projected, or that somehow things will just work out.

"Count Every Penny"

On the other hand, even though most retirees say that longevity is their biggest concern, recent surveys have repeatedly shown that retirees are NOT spending down their assets but rather cutting back in lifestyle for fear of running out. The mounting worry leads them to sacrifice the retirement they envisioned.

Based on these two extremities, I have found the lifestyle concern to be the biggest of the five concerns. It can be a dangerous choice to make: maintain your desired overall standard of living or be forced to make moderate to drastic lifestyle changes.

Regardless of the components, lifestyle goals can be revealing when it comes to your expectations. How concerning is Lifestyle to you? Answer this question.

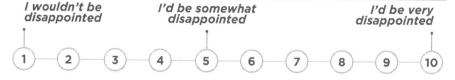

On a scale of 1 to 10, how disappointed would you be if you had to adjust your standard of living to make your savings last? (Circle your number)

I wouldn't be disappointed	I'd be somewhat disappointed	I'd be very disappointed

1   2   3   4   5   6   7   8   9   10

The Liquidity Question

Will I have access to money when I need it?

Maintaining additional assets that can be tapped quickly to provide funds for unexpected contingencies is critical in retirement. Ideally, these reserves should be accessible with as little taxable impact as possible to provide for things like emergencies, run-of-the-mill spending shocks, expenses or perhaps retirement enjoyment. These expenses are items that you need (or want) to buy but don't want to liquidate savings to do it.

The "what ifs" of retirement are endless and having access to a reserve for the inevitable is essential. To determine your liquidity tolerance, answer this question:

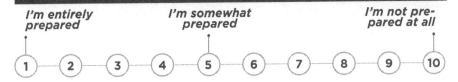

On a scale of 1 to 10, how prepared would you be for unexpected spending shocks in retirement? (Circle your number)

I'm entirely prepared   *I'm somewhat prepared*   *I'm not prepared at all*

1 — 2 — 3 — 4 — 5 — 6 — 7 — 8 — 9 — 10

The Legacy Question

How will I be financially remembered?

Legacy is more than just money. Think about the financial memories you have of your loved ones. Dad was a saver who always said to save a dime from every dollar. Grandmom was a spender. Uncle Bill drank up all of his money. Grandpa lived through the depression and was always wary of the stock market.

Traditional legacy goals relate to leaving assets for future generations, or to charities, and no doubt, this is great when it can happen. However, legacy also includes how you were able to manage your finances, especially during the retirement years. Did you find it necessary to borrow money from your children, move in with one of them, or ask another to adjust their work schedule to take care of your medical needs?

Preparing for your legacy involves more than just money. How would you answer this question?

On a scale of 1 to 10, how important is it to you to leave a financial legacy? (Circle your number)

It's not important   *It's somewhat important*   *It's very important*

1 — 2 — 3 — 4 — 5 — 6 — 7 — 8 — 9 — 10

The Long-Term Care Question

Am I financially prepared for the costs of health-related expenses?

Long-term care involves a variety of services designed to meet a person's health or personal care needs during a short or long period of time. These services help people with chronic, disabling, or otherwise, serious health conditions live as independently and safely as possible when they can no longer perform everyday activities on their own - basic functions (e.g., eating, bathing), household work (e.g., meal preparation, shopping), and medical/nursing tasks.

The out-of-pocket costs for health-related expenses is the single biggest overlooked and underfunded expense in retirement. A 2018 study by Fidelity Investments said that a couple retiring that year would need an estimated $280,000 to cover out-of-pocket healthcare costs in retirement.

This estimate applies to those with traditional Medicare insurance coverage and considers premiums, co-payments, deductibles, and out-of-pocket drug costs. It does not consider the cost of a nursing home or long-term care (estimated to be an additional $130,000). These costs are real and ignored almost completely.

Here then is the question:

Longevity, lifestyle, liquidity, legacy and long-term care are all challenges that must be addressed when developing even the most basic retirement income plan. Now let's explore how a plan that includes housing wealth may mitigate your retirement risks, meet these challenges head-on, and give you the peace of mind you deserve.

Five Client Questions:

How much does the thought of running out of savings in retirement trouble you?

How prepared are you for unexpected spending shocks in retirement?

How disappointed would you be if you had to adjust your standard of living in order to make your savings last?

How important is it to you to leave a financial legacy?

How prepared would you be if you had to access an additional $300,000 for health care related costs?

5

What Can Housing Wealth Do for Your Retirement?

So far, we've discovered the types of retirement challenges you're facing and clarified your most pressing concerns. Now we ask the question: what can Housing Wealth do for your retirement income plan?

Before we delve into that answer, let's look at the existing assets, or resources, that most retirees have at their disposal.

Three Buckets of Retirement Wealth: Income, Investments, Insurances

For years, retirees have had three primary sources of wealth to work with in creating a retirement income plan:

- The Income Bucket (Social Security, pension, employment, etc.)

- The Investment Bucket (IRA, 401k, 403b, CD's, Money Market, etc.)

- The Insurance Bucket (annuities, life insurance, business to be sold, second home, etc.)

It was from these available sources that retirees and their advisors sought to create lifetime income while attempting to lessen risk and maintain their desired lifestyle. But in modern times, are these three buckets of wealth and traditional planning tools enough to create the retirement you deserve?

In my experience, the answer is no. Retirees are living longer and have not saved nearly enough to maintain the type of retirement they desire. The good news is there is an additional bucket that's easily accessible to most retirees: Home Equity.

The Fourth Bucket: Home Equity

Make no mistake, the presence of home equity in retirement is significant.

- Currently, there is more than 6 trillion dollars in senior home equity.
- 87 percent of baby boomers and existing retirees own their home.
- U.S. Census Bureau states that the average retiring 65-year-old couple will have 68 percent of their total wealth tied up in their home equity.

Equity and Non-Equity Assets

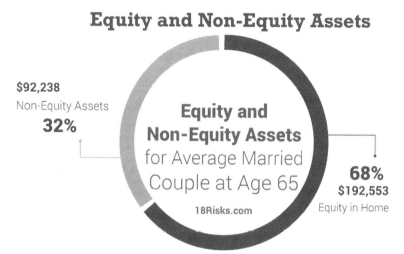

$92,238
Non-Equity Assets
32%

Equity and Non-Equity Assets for Average Married Couple at Age 65

18Risks.com

68%
$192,553
Equity in Home

Simply stated, the average retiree is living in their biggest asset and most significant source of their total wealth.

Think about this in the context of the current retirement savings and longevity crisis; doesn't considering home equity in a retirement income plan just make sense?

Using Home Equity in Retirement Is Not Really New

Did you realize the home has been used in the retirement conversation for years?

You see, using the home as a retirement planning tool has been around for as long as most of us have been alive. The reverse mortgage is no different; it was developed in response to major shifts in the retirement landscape and the new, significant challenges that previous generations did not face. It's simply an age-appropriate, equity-release strategy.

Product	Ideal Life Season	Purpose
30-Year Mortgage	Ages 25 - 50	Using the bank's money versus your own money to purchase an appreciating asset that will be used as an investment later for a variety of planning purposes. In this strategy, you make monthly repayments over time - reducing the loan balance and increasing the home's equity. These payments are like forced savings that allow you to begin accumulating retirement assets (the home, primarily) for future use.
Home Equity Loans and Lines of Credit	Ages 40 - 65	Borrowing from the home's equity to meet certain needs or fund projects versus using savings - allowing savings to grow for retirement.
Downsizing/ Rightsizing	Ages 55 - 75	Selling the existing home and using the remaining proceeds (if enough) to buy a different home or rent an apartment. This often allows retirees to generate new retirement savings, lower their expenses, or accomplish both.
Reverse Mortgages	Ages 65 - 90	Converting the home's equity into tax-free income without the requirement of monthly mortgage payments. The program can also be used to purchase a new home without taking on a new mortgage payment or borrowing from savings.

And when equity is released for the retiree, it turns into what we call Housing Wealth! Housing Wealth (via the reverse mortgage) is the unlocked and guaranteed access to the appreciating equity in your home without the requirement of a monthly mortgage payment.

With the reverse mortgage's restructuring and the recent academic research supporting its use, it can now play the role it was created to play: helping retirees access and use their Housing Wealth to create a more enjoyable retirement.

The Value of a Well-Informed Advisor

Research shows that retirement outcomes are clearly strengthened with the presence of a skilled advisor and a written plan. However, not every advisor considers Housing Wealth when developing retirement income plans.

The 4 Buckets

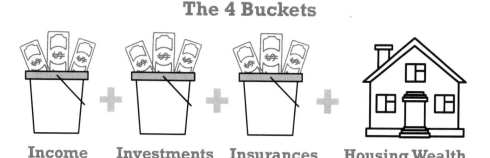

Income   Investments   Insurances   Housing Wealth

Given the information just presented and the strategies yet to be discussed, I strongly recommend working with an advisor who has at least a cursory knowledge of how reverse mortgages work.

Ideally, you would find an advisor who knows how to skillfully incorporate reverse mortgages with the rest of your retirement assets to create different options and outcomes for you to consider.

Understandably, not every advisor knows how to do this or has time to go beyond the basics of reverse mortgages. The Housing Wealth Certificate Course was designed to help advisors who would like to discover more. You can find out more at www.HousingWealthInstitute.com

Three Next Steps

Incorporating all available assets into a retirement planning conversation can often make a significant difference in your outcomes and peace of mind. Throughout the rest of this book, we'll unpack why the newly restructured reverse mortgage may be a particularly useful tool for you to unlock your home equity and put your housing wealth to its best use.

Here are the steps we'll follow:

- ☐ **Step 1:** Get the Basics - Myths and Misconception About How the Reverse Mortgage Works

- ☐ **Step 2**: Learn the Foundational Strategies - Five Ways to Incorporate Reverse Mortgages

- ☐ **Step 3:** Evaluate If It's Right for You

SECTION 2:

THE NEWLY
RESTRUCTURED
REVERSE MORTGAGE

6

Reverse Mortgages 101

The Family Picnic

Has this ever had this happened to you?

You're at a family gathering and someone mentions they're thinking about getting a reverse mortgage.

Some family members may sheepishly excuse themselves - sensing the approach of a conversation they'd rather avoid. A few will say, "I've heard about those," and may be open to hearing more, while others may be much more outspoken. Still others will have questions they won't verbalize such as these:

> **"Did they lose their money to a poor investment? It must be pretty bad if it's come to this."**

> **"I thought these things were for poor people who don't have savings, and I know they have several hundred thousand dollars saved."**

> **"There goes the inheritance."**

Over the past two decades, I have heard similar concerns from many well-meaning clients, friends, and even financial professionals.

Here are a few other concerns people have expressed:

√ **Too Controversial:** "They have a lot of bad press, and it seems that when they do come up, the response is always negative."

√ **Too Complicated:** "They have too many bells, whistles, and hidden trap doors. I don't know anyone who understands them."

√ **Too Expensive:** "I hear the costs can be high."

√ **Not for My Clients:** "Even if they did ask, my clients would never have a need for one."

√ **Products That Should Only Be Used a Last Resort:** "I would only tell my friend/client to do one if they ran out of money and it was the last possible option."

There is no doubt that you have heard some of these concerns or had them yourself. Honestly, each of them has an element of truth. However, what you will discover is that the concerns on that list are either outdated, exaggerated, or misunderstood. In the coming pages, we will unpack them and share honest and straightforward answers to each.

Four Simple Words

Over the years, I have discovered that sharing four words about reverse mortgages can help put everyone at ease:

IT'S JUST A MORTGAGE!

Here's a fun quiz to help me illustrate.

Who Had the Reverse Mortgage?

 Two couples in their early 60s need some home renovations and want to take a nice vacation.

Both sets of couples:

- Decide a home equity loan is best
- Go to a lender.
- Produce income and credit qualifications.
- Are approved for $100,000 line of credit.
- Use the money.

- Are required to maintain their home and pay taxes and homeowner's insurance.
- Make the exact same monthly payments.
- Have their loan balance decrease until paid off.

One couple got a reverse mortgage and the other couple got a traditional home equity loan. Can you tell the difference?

Of course not, that's the point. On the surface reverse mortgages share the same basic features as traditional loan products: you have a need, want a loan, produce documents to qualify, get approved, make payments, and call it a day!

To be certain, reverse mortgages do have some distinctive features we'll discuss in this chapter, but underneath the surface, **it's just a mortgage!**

Reverse Mortgage History

Equity release programs for seniors have been in existence for more than 100 years. After starting in England, they spread to numerous countries including Scotland, Ireland, China, Singapore, Australia, Indonesia, New Zealand, Canada, and beyond. Regardless of their location in the world, the basic premise has always been the same: help an aging population sustain a longer retirement.

We've already covered the basic housing wealth options:

 Sell the home, take out the cash, and move.

 Take out a traditional home equity loan and make monthly payments.

These choices have value, but they don't always meet the needs of retirees who want to stay in their home and NOT have to make monthly mortgage payments. Enter the equity release program - a way to convert the home asset into retirement income. No moving or mandatory monthly payments involved. In the United States, these programs are called reverse mortgages, and there are four primary types that exist today:

Private Reverse Mortgages. These began in 1961.

Jumbo Reverse Mortgages. These are private equity release programs for higher-value or second homes. Typically, homes that benefit most from these are worth 1 million dollars or more.

The Home Equity Conversion Mortgage (HECM). In existence since 1988, these reverse mortgages are overseen by the U.S. Department of Housing and Urban Development (HUD) and are insured by the Federal Housing Administration (FHA). Today, nearly 95 percent of all reverse mortgages are HECMs.

The HECM for Purchase. This loan allows retirees to purchase a new home with the proceeds of the HECM financing a portion of the purchase price. A new home can be purchased for about 50 to 60 percent down with no monthly mortgage payments.

Understanding the Basics

For the sake of our discussion, we're going to focus on the Home Equity Conversion Mortgage (HECM). It is a federally insured, non-recourse loan that allows people age sixty-two or older to convert a portion of the equity of their primary residence into tax-free dollars.

What are the age eligibility qualifications?

To qualify, at least one borrowing spouse must be age sixty-two or older. A younger partner is considered a Non-Borrowing Spouse and need only be over eighteen.

What type of properties qualify?

The HECM can only be done on the retiree's primary residence. The property can be a single-family home, a HUD-approved condo, a manufactured home, or a one to four-unit home with the condition that the retiree lives in one of the four units.

Do you give up ownership or come off title to the home?

The borrower never gives up ownership of the home or comes off title.

Are there financial/credit qualifications?

Borrowers need to prove their willingness and capacity to meet their monthly obligations: property-related taxes, insurance, and any monthly mortgage payments. These must have been paid in a timely manner over the past twenty-four to thirty-six months. If they were not, the lender will request letters of explanation, proof of extenuating circumstances, or require that tax and insurance payments be set aside from loan proceeds and be paid automatically.

Furthermore, borrowers must have a certain amount of monthly income leftover after covering their basic housing obligations. If they don't, the lender may consider accumulated savings satisfactory, or they may count a portion of the HECM loan funds to cover any shortfall.

Does the home need to be free and clear?

A HECM must be a first mortgage. This means if you have a remaining mortgage or home equity loan balance, you are required to pay it prior to settlement, or use the HECM proceeds to pay it off before using the money in any other way.

Triangle Basics
Calculating the HECM Benefit

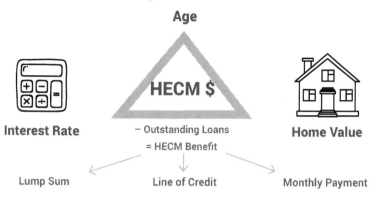

Age

Interest Rate

HECM $

− Outstanding Loans
= HECM Benefit

Home Value

Lump Sum   Line of Credit   Monthly Payment

How much can borrowers qualify for?

The amount of money a borrower is eligible for is based on three primary factors:

- **Age** of the youngest borrower
- **Value** of the property, up to the current lending limit ($726,525 at time of printing)
- **Interest rate** associated with the selected program

How can proceeds be distributed?

There are five ways in which you can receive your HECM proceeds:

- **Lump Sum:** As a protective feature, the borrower can only receive 60 percent of available benefit in the first year. The remainder can be received in subsequent years.
- **Line of Credit:** Similar to a home equity line of credit, you can tap into a pool of money as needed. However, unlike the traditional home equity loan, this reserve increases over time.
- **Regular Tenure Payments:** This is a regular monthly payment backed by the federal government and guaranteed to come to the borrower for as long as the loan is open.
- **Regular Term Payments:** A monthly payment of a set amount is received over a specific amount of time.
- **Hybrid:** This option is a combination of a lump sum (often used to pay off a mortgage) and monthly payments, with the line of credit functioning as a reserve.

You can get an approximate idea of how much you may receive through a HECM by using one of the many reverse mortgage online calculators. A very simple calculator that does not require email, phone number, or personal information can be found at www.HousingWealthCalculator.com

Do you have to make a monthly mortgage payment?

There are no mandatory monthly loan repayments required.

Is third party counseling a requirement for reverse mortgages?

Reverse mortgage counseling is a mandatory requirement of the application process and is typically completed before an application for a reverse mortgage loan is taken. HUD certifies and approves reverse mortgage counselors around the country to provide home-owners with impartial education about reverse mortgage loans. This counseling can be performed face-to-face or by telephone.

Does the borrower have any requirements?

There are four basic requirements the borrower must do to maintain the HECM reverse mortgage:

- The home must remain the **principal residence** of at least one of the borrowers. You can own more than one residence but only the primary residence can have a HECM in place.

- The home **must be maintained** in a lendable condition. For example, the borrower cannot allow a tree to fall through the roof and not get the roof repaired.

- Borrower must keep basic **homeowners' insurance** in force.

- Borrower must pay all **property-related taxes.**

How Did Reverse Mortgages Get Such a Bad Reputation?

If those are the only requirements for maintaining the loan, why do they often get bad press? Just watch the latest news broadcast: Elderly Woman Gets Put Out of Home Over $0.27 in Reverse Mortgage. Or read the latest newspaper heading: Retired Couple Loses Home to Reverse Mortgage.

What do you think is the number one reason the program ends up in the media with stories like those?

If you said borrowers not paying their property taxes, you would be correct.

What you'll find in nearly every case is the homeowners did not, would not or, in some cases, could not pay their property-related taxes. When this happens, it is the municipality who initiates action and informs the lender, who is then forced to act. It's the same thing that would happen with any type of mortgage.

Fortunately, the U.S. Department of Housing and Urban Development (HUD) has created a tremendous improvement over the last few years. With the Reverse Mortgage Stabilization Act of 2013, the 2015 Financial Assessment, and the 2017 HECM overhaul, most of the earlier challenges have been addressed by:

- **Greater Spousal Protection.** A younger spouse can remain on title and does not face displacement if the older spouse predeceases them.

- **Greater Equity Protections.** The new HUD overhaul benefits clients by reducing interest rates, so the loan grows more slowly and preserves more equity, while still making sufficient initial dollars available.

- **Greater Scrutiny of Income and Credit**. The goal is to make sure the right retirees - those with a pattern of financial responsibility who understand the program's purpose - are given access to the program.

Unfortunately, there is no safeguard for irresponsible borrowers, the occasional misguided lender, or the rogue advisor, but the strengthening of the program and public accountability have gone a long way to make reverse mortgages a viable addition to retirement income plans.

When Does the Loan Get Repaid?

The HECM does not have to be repaid until the last surviving homeowner either passes away or permanently moves from the property. Borrowers cannot be forced by a lender to sell their home (for the purpose of repayment) as long as the loan requirements are met, and they can remain in their home for as long as they like, even if the outstanding loan balance, plus interest, is more than the value of the property.

When the home is no longer being used as a primary residence, the cash advances, interest, and other finance charges related to the reverse mortgage must be repaid to the lender. ALL remaining proceeds, beyond the amount that is owed, belong to the borrower, or the estate if the borrower is deceased. In the case of the borrower's death, the remaining equity can then be transferred to the heirs. NO debt is passed along to the beneficiaries.

In most cases, the home is sold, but if the family wishes to retain the home, they can use whatever means available to repay the lender, including life Insurance, other assets, or refinancing the HECM into a traditional loan.

HUD requires the repayment conversation to be initiated with the lender/servicer within thirty days of the last surviving borrower's permanent departure from the home. The executor will then have six months to settle the HECM. Extensions can be granted by HUD for an additional six months.

Repayment Example

- Borrower Age: 70
- Home Value: **$200,000**
- HECM Proceeds: **$100,000** at an interest rate of 5 percent
- Outstanding Beginning Balance: **$100,000**

Day One: Borrowers' home is worth $200,000. They obtained a HECM and paid off their existing mortgage. After settlement, they now owe the HECM lender $100,000.

If they were to move or decease at the end of week one, the home would be sold and the $100,000 (plus one week's worth of interest)

HECM Reverse Mortgage Repayment

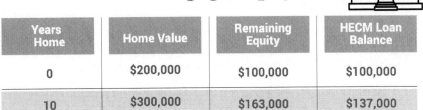

Years Home	Home Value	Remaining Equity	HECM Loan Balance
0	$200,000	$100,000	$100,000
10	$300,000	$163,000	$137,000

is owed. The remaining $100,000 will go to them if they move or pass on to the heirs/estate if the borrower has deceased.

Ten Years Later: If the borrower stayed in the home for ten years and chose not to make monthly payments, the interest on the loan will have accrued, and their loan balance will be larger. On the chart, notice that in year ten, they owe the lender $163,000.

The chart also shows the $200,000 home appreciating at about 4 percent over those ten years. It's now worth $300,000. If they were to move or decease at this time, the home could be sold, the HECM paid off, and they (or their heirs) pocket the difference of $137,000.

How much will the borrowers owe in years fifteen, twenty, and twenty-five?

We may not know exactly what will happen in the future, but for this illustration, we will assume the loan balance has grown to $400,000. Let's see what happens with three different future home values.

Home Value	Loan Balance	Retained Equity
$600,000	$400,000	$200,000
$500,000	$400,000	$100,000
$400,000	$400,000	$0
$300,000	$400,000	$0 FHA insures borrower and protects heirs/estate

You see in the last column, the home's value is $300,000, but the loan balance is $400,000. This means the borrower (upon their death or departure) owes more than the home is worth. What happens?

What does a non-recourse loan mean?

Since the HECM reverse mortgage is an FHA insured, non-recourse loan, the lender's ONLY "recourse" is the net proceeds from the sale of the home ($300,000), even though the client owes $400,000.

The FHA Mortgage Insurance Fund bridges the difference so that neither the client nor their estate/heirs are responsible for repayment of the note, and no deficiency judgment can be taken.

There is often a world of difference between what people believe about the reverse mortgage and what it actually is.

To be fair, I have found that most of the information people have accumulated on the topic is simply outdated. That's why I'm so glad you have decided to set apart a little time to learn the facts and to separate myth from reality.

Here's a short fact vs. myth quiz to prepare you for the next time reverse mortgages come up in discussion.

1. The Home Equity Conversion Mortgage is the legal name of the FHA insured reverse mortgage program.

a. True

b. False

2. The earliest age at which a person who is the sole-owner of a home can enter into a reverse mortgage is 55.

a. True

b. False

3. One downside of entering into a reverse mortgage is that the bank takes title and ownership of the home.

a. True

b. False

4. A reverse mortgage can be used to purchase a home.

a. True

b. False

5. A reverse mortgage can be used to refinance or to pay off an existing mortgage, and the borrower is not required to make monthly mortgage payments as long as he or she is still using the home as the principal residence.

a. True

b. False

6. Once you enter into a reverse mortgage, you no longer have to pay property taxes or homeowners insurance.

a. True

b. False

7. If a borrower takes out a reverse mortgage and the home is later goes "underwater" (the home is worth less than the amount owed to the lender), the homeowner, estate, or heirs would need to pay off the additional debt to the bank at the end of the loan.

a. True

b. False

8. The four different types of reverse mortgages that exist today are (1) Jumbo, (2) Private, (3) HECMs, and (4) HECM for Purchase.

a. True

b. False

9. If both borrowers decease, 100% of any remaining proceeds from the home go to the heirs or estate after the reverse mortgage balance is paid off.

a. True

b. False

10. Reverse mortgage proceeds can be taken as a lump sum, in a line of credit, as monthly payments, or a combination of all of the above.

a. True

b. False

Answers:

1. **True** – the Home Equity Conversion Mortgage is the legal government name since 1988.

2. **False** – At least one borrowing spouse must be age 62.

3. **False** – The borrower never gives up ownership of the home or comes off title.

4. **True** – The HECM for Purchase program can be used to buy a home.

5. **True** – A reverse mortgage must be a first mortgage. If a mortgage or home equity loan balance remains, it must be paid off. There are NO mandatory monthly payments required.

6. **False** – There are four borrower requirements: (1) home must remain the principal residence and (2) be maintained in a lendable condition. (3) Basic homeowner's insurance must be kept in force and (4) all property-related taxes must be paid.

7. **False** – The HECM reverse mortgage is an FHA insured, non-recourse loan. Neither the client nor their heirs/estate are responsible for paying more than the value of the home.

8. **True** – The four primary types of reverse mortgages are Jumbo, Private, HECM and HECM for Purchase.

9. **True** – After the loan is paid off, 100% of any remaining proceeds go to the borrower (if they have moved) or to their heirs/estate if they have deceased.

10. **True** – The combination option usually includes a lump sum used to pay off a mortgage and a line of credit functioning as a reserve (that can be converted to monthly payments).

Next Steps

Congratulations, you now know more about reverse mortgages than the vast majority of your peers.

Next up, the five foundational strategies. This is where things start getting exciting. You're about to see exactly how the reverse mortgage can meet your specific retirement concerns.

√ **Step 1:** Get the Basics: Myths and Misconception About How the Reverse Mortgage Works

☐ **Step 2:** Learn the Foundational Strategies: Five Ways to Incorporate Reverse Mortgages

☐ **Step 3:** Evaluate If It's Right for You

SECTION 3:

THE FIVE FOUNDATIONS OF HOUSING WEALTH

> "You can't build a great building on a weak foundation. You must have a solid foundation if you're going to have a strong superstructure." - Gordon B. Hinckley

Earlier we discovered the newly restructured reverse mortgage is designed to help retirees Increase Cash Flow, Reduce Risks, Preserve Assets, Improve Liquidity and Add New Dollars back into retirement savings.

In this section, I will cover how these outcomes can be achieved with the five core HECM foundations, or strategies.

HECM Line of Credit | HECM Monthly Payment | HECM Replacement | HECM Exchange | HECM for Purchase

I encourage you to read the following chapters in order as some of the strategies build on one another.

7

The HECM Line of Credit Strategy

What if I told you that you could turn a portion of your home's equity into a tax-free reserve fund that has a built-in, guaranteed growth rate? That it couldn't be frozen, canceled, or reduced and could be accessed at any time in the future, regardless of your home's value, income, assets, or credit - what would you say?

What I'm describing is the Reverse Mortgage Line of Credit (ReLOC), or what I like to call the 8th wonder of the financial world.

How Does the Line of Credit Work?

Most of us are familiar with a traditional banking line of credit, or a something like a Visa, Mastercard, or Discover credit card. They all work in a similar way. The bank/credit card company gives you the ability to borrow money (up to a limit) and then repay those advances over time.

The reverse mortgage line of credit works similarly, but with a few significant differences:

√ **No Monthly Payments** The ReLOC does NOT require any monthly loan payments on the money that is taken.

√ **Line of Credit Growth** The unused portion of the ReLOC actually grows! It has a built-in, guaranteed growth factor that allows it to grow regardless of the home's value! This means you can secure a ReLOC and access more dollars down the road than what it was originally worth.

The chart shows the projected growth of the ReLOC for a 62-year-old with $200,000, $400,000, and $600,000 home values.

Year	$200,000 ReLOC Value	$400,000 ReLOC Value	$600,000 ReLOC Value
0	$79,396	$162,796	$248,196
5	$103,118	$211,437	$322,353
10	$133,929	$274,611	$418,668
15	$173,945	$356,661	$543,760
20	$225,917	$463,227	$706,227
25	$309,167	$633,926	$966,472
30	$381,086	$781,391	$1,191,295

What Is the Difference Between a Traditional Line of Credit and the HECM Line of Credit?

The chart below shows more of the differences between a standard home equity line of credit and the reverse mortgage line of credit. (Please assume that the total costs and fees for both products are about the same.)

The HECM line of credit is clearly different and uniquely designed with the retiree in mind. Another way to think of it is as **Equity Insurance.**

Most retirees are already paying for at least two types of insurance - homeowners and auto - even though the probability of using those insurance policies and recouping their investment is low.

HELOC	ReLOC
Access to the line for ten years	No mandatory ten-year draw
Must make minimum monthly payments	No minimum payments required
Lender can freeze or cancel loan amounts	Lender cannot freeze or cancel loan amounts
Home subject to foreclosure if minimum payments, insurance, and taxes are not paid	Home subject to foreclosure if insurance and taxes are not paid
Loan balance must be paid back in full, even if the borrower owes more than the home is worth	Borrowers or heirs never pay back more than the home's fair market value when sold

It may also be wise to add Equity Insurance or the guaranteed access to the appreciating equity in your home without the burden of a mandatory payment when accessed. This is because the probability of needing a reserve fund in retirement is very likely and having access to a growing fund of dollars (independent of the home's value) is ideal.

Let's take a look at how some retirees are making use of their equity insurance.

Bob and Sally Are Retiring

Bob (68) is retired and Sally (66) works part-time and is retiring soon.

Traditional Line of Credit: Over the last 30 years, Bob and Sally have always had some sort of home equity loan or line of credit to draw on for enjoyment and expenses. It started when one of their kids needed financial help finishing college and then they used it to pay for their daughter's wedding. They also consolidated some high-interest credit card debt, upgraded the kitchen, and took a longer than usual vacation across Europe, amongst other things.

Bob and Sally were smart to leave their retirement savings alone and use their home equity instead. They made payments after each use and then if necessary, acquired a new line of credit and started again. It worked great for them, and they appreciated having a reserve.

Retiree's Line of Credit: As they enter retirement, things begin to change, and they start to rely on accumulated savings and Social Security.

Bob and Sally still want the flexibility of a home equity reserve, but they no longer want the burden of a mandatory monthly payment when they use it. They heard from some friends about a reverse mortgage line of credit. As they did their own research, they felt that this type of reverse mortgage would be the perfect replacement for their traditional home equity line of credit because it gives them their desired reserve fund without the mandatory payments.

They also saw the benefit to having a growing line of credit that couldn't be frozen, canceled, or reduced. If it's a good month and they can afford to make a payment on it, they will, but the pressure is off knowing they don't have to!

What Are Other Ways to Use the HECM Line of Credit?

Replace a Home Equity Line of Credit: That's what Bob and Sally just did!

Inflation Protection: Inflation simply means products and goods are more expensive over time. As mentioned earlier, this can have a devastating effect on retirement. When inflation rates are high, a retiree's savings don't go as far and more money must be pulled from the portfolio - eroding it more quickly. Because the standard reverse mortgage line of credit is growing today between 5-6%, it is outpacing inflation. This can give you a measure of comfort - knowing that at least one of your assets is expected to keep pace with inflation.

Protect Against Declining Property Values and Unexpected Expenses: Have you ever considered that your home could decline in value, or that the economy could experience another housing bubble where prices collapse? What happens if you need to access money from your home but circumstances out of your control prevent you from obtaining a traditional home equity loan or line of credit? The ReLOC is desirable because it guarantees you access to an appreciating line of credit (1) even if the home's value declines and (2) even if the ReLOC available balance is greater than the home's value.

Protect Your Portfolio: Sometimes, a portfolio may decline significantly in value. When this happens, a retiree can borrow from the ReLOC to cover expenses instead of locking in the loss by drawing from their portfolio. Then, if they'd like, they can repay the loan and replenish the line of credit when the portfolio recovers. This strategy is outlined in chapter 14.

Pay Roth Conversion Taxes: Although tax-free retirement income is very desirable, it's not always achievable. Many retirees already know that converting a portion of their taxable savings to a tax-free Roth IRA is a great strategy. However, there's often an obstacle that stands in their way: the amount of income taxes owed on the converted amount. In chapter 17, we will see how the HECM line of credit can be used to seamlessly fund the Roth Conversion.

Is There an Optimal Time to Establish the Line of Credit?

We've seen that the ReLOC is a valuable retirement tool with numerous uses. Now the question is: when is the best time to set it up?

This was the question that began to emerge in 2012 as many financial thought leaders took notice of the power and versatility of the ReLOC.

The consensus was that if the average retiree was planning to stay in their home, then setting a line of credit earlier in retirement was optimal. The simple reason being that by starting early you give the line of credit a chance to grow and compound in such a way that if you started later, though the starting amount may be greater, it would never catch up to where the earlier ReLOC had grown.

A Tale of Three Lines

In the following chart, Dr. Wade Pfau, professor of retirement income at the American College and nationally recognized retirement thought leader (www.retirementresearcher.com) graphically shows the value of establishing a HECM line of credit sooner rather than later.

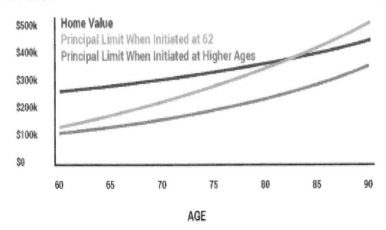

The top line shows the value of the home appreciating over time.

The middle line shows a retiree establishing a ReLOC at the onset of retirement and allowing it to grow.

The bottom line shows a client waiting to establish a ReLOC until later in retirement. In theory, by doing this the loan benefit would be greater because the client is older, and the home is worth more, but as the chart shows, the odds that the delayed line would catch up with the earlier are pretty slim.

The research is clear. If you are a retiree and planning to remain in your home, then establishing the line of credit sooner than later may be a prudent strategy to consider.

The reverse mortgage line of credit is not only the 8th wonder of the financial world but also the swiss army knife of retirement planning. Its versatility makes it perhaps one of the most important tools in your retirement toolbox.

EQUITY INSURANCE: Guaranteed access to the appreciating equity in your home, without the burden of a mandatory payment when it is accessed.

8

The HECM Monthly Payment Strategy

One of the key benefits of the Home Equity Conversion Mortgage is that you can receive the proceeds in any way you choose. We've considered the value in having access to an appreciating line of credit. Another way you can receive the reverse mortgage funds is by converting all or some of the remaining line of credit into monthly payments.

Many of us are used to having money deposited into our bank accounts month-by-month, so this can be a familiar and preferable way to receive the proceeds. Let's explore the two types of monthly payments that allow you to employ dynamic strategies to strengthen your retirement plan.

The Tenure Payment

The first type of monthly payment is called the Tenure payment. Based on your age, the value of your home, and current interest rates, the lender determines the maximum amount you can receive each month for the entire duration of the loan.

These payments, insured by the Federal Housing Administration of the U.S. Department of Housing and Urban Development, are guaranteed to come to you for as long as you maintain the terms of the loan (live in and maintain the property, pay your property related taxes, and keep homeowner's insurance in force).

The Term Payment

A variation of the monthly payment is called a Term Payment. This is designed for a scenario in which you don't want, or need, a monthly payment for an indefinite amount of time - only for a fixed period such as 5 or 10 years.

The following charts compare the amounts a retiree can receive based on home values of $200,000; $400,000; and $600,000.

(Column A) HECM Line of Credit

(Column B) Tenure Payment

(Column C) 5-Year Term Payment

(Column D) 10-Year Term Payment

Age 65 | $200,000 Home Value | 5% Expected Rate

Age	A	B	C	D
	LOC Amount	Tenure Pmt	5-yr Term	10-yr Term
65	$76,000	$406	$1,445	$821
70	$99,993	$565	$1,901	$1,080
75	$131,562	$804	$2,502	$1,421
80	$173,096	$1,185	$3,291	$1,870
85	$227,744	$1,852	$4,330	$2,460
90	$299,643	$3,237	$5,697	n/a

Age 65 | $400,000 Home Value | 5% Expected Rate

Age	A	B	C	D
	LOC Amount	Tenure Pmt	5-yr Term	10-yr Term
65	$154,000	$823	$2,928	$1,664
70	$202,618	$1,145	$3,853	$2,189
75	$266,586	$1,630	$5,069	$2,880
80	$350,748	$2,402	$6,669	$3,789
85	$461,480	$3,753	$8,775	$4,985
90	$607,171	$6,559	$11,545	$6,559

Age 65 | $600,000 Home Value | 5% Expected Rate

Age	A	B	C	D
	LOC Amount	Tenure Pmt	5-yr Term	10-yr Term
65	$234,000	$1,251	$4,449	$2,528
70	$307,875	$1,740	$5,854	$3,326
75	$405,072	$2,476	$7,702	$4,376
80	$532,955	$3,649	$10,134	$5,758
85	$701,210	$5,703	$13,333	$7,575
90	$922,585	$9,967	$17,542	$9,967

Notice that in each case, the unused portion of the line of credit grows but at any time you can convert that line of credit into a monthly Tenure Payment or Term Payment.

For example, if the retiree in the $400,000 home, waited 5 years (until age 70) and then converted to a tenure payment, their line of credit has grown ($202,618) making their available tenure payment greater as well ($1,145). If they wait another 5 years (age 75), they will receive $1,630 per month, and so on.

8 Strategic Uses of the Term and Tenure Payments

There are a host of creative ways that monthly payments can be utilized, here are a few ideas.

(1) Budgeted Living vs. Desired Living: There is a real danger of overspending in retirement due in part to the distinct retirement phases and how much retirees tend to spend in each phase: Go-Go Years, Slow-Go Years, and No-Go Years.

My friend, Tom Hegna, retirement income leader, author, and host of PBS special "Don't Worry, Retire Happy" describes the three phases like this:

"A lot of people think retirement is going to be thirty to forty years of golf, tennis, cruises, and line dancing. I tell people that's not true. You are going to go through three distinct phases.

The first phase is what I call the Go-Go years. Now, during the Go-Go years, you are playing golf, you are playing tennis, you are going on cruises, you are line dancing, and every day it's happy hour somewhere.

But make no mistake about it; the Go-Go years are going to be followed by the Slow-Go years. Now, during the Slow-Go years, you can still do everything you did in the Go-Go years, you just don't want to anymore. In fact, you don't want to go downtown after 4:30pm because Dad can't see when it's dark out. That's the Slow-Go years.

And the Slow-Go years are going to be followed by the No-Go years. The No-Go years are those years where you are probably not leaving the building until you're leaving the building if you know what I am talking about."

Often retirees have a monthly budget that is designed to sustain them for all of retirement, but it can sometimes leave them lacking income or enjoyment each month. Take a look at the illustration and notice the two lines. The top line is the desired spending, and the second line is the budgeted spending.

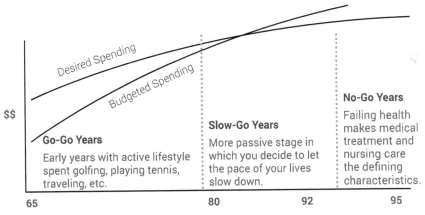

Usually, at the onset of retirement, there is a larger gap between desired spending and budgeted spending. This is when you want to spend $100 a week for golf, but your wife reminds you of the budget; or when you want to go on a short vacation, but your husband reminds you of the budget!

This dilemma can cause retirees to make choices with very serious consequences. One choice may be to go ahead and spend beyond their budget and hope that somehow things work out: investments perform better than expected, don't live as long as projected, etc.

A possible solution is converting the reverse mortgage into monthly payments. This option would increase the amount retirees could spend monthly - giving them more enjoyment. It could also reduce the draw on their savings - allowing savings to last longer.

(2) Social Security Deferral: Most retirees know that deferring Social Security for as long as possible leads to a much higher payout (See chart). This is a particularly good strategy for the higher wage earner, especially if you believe you will live beyond age 78.

However, some simply need the money at 62 and don't have another resource to supplement all or part of their income while they wait. They can establish a reverse mortgage and schedule monthly payments to cover the shortfall for a certain number of years. HECM term payments can provide an income bridge to allow retirees to delay claiming Social Security until benefits are worth the maximum amount at age 70.

Social Security and Retirement Income Optimization

Monthly Benefit Amount by Age you Decide to Start Receiving Benefits
This example assumes a benefit of $1,000 at a full retirement age of 66

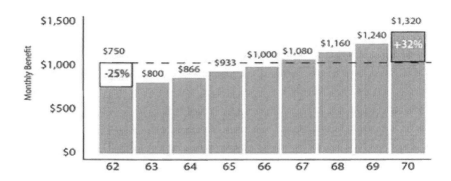

(3) Qualified Plan Maximization (IRA/401k): Similarly, creating an income can allow retirees to defer taking their qualified savings

(IRAs, 401k, etc.) until they reach minimum distribution age (70 ½). This allows the funds to continue to grow tax-deferred and, presumably, create a larger benefit when mandatory withdrawals are required.

(4) Vesting for Annuity Pay-Out: One of the benefits of a deferred annuity is its ability to grow and upon annuitization, have a larger monthly payout. This is called vesting. Although most annuities will allow you to convert to a monthly payment at any time, there is a significant benefit to leaving the funds alone for the recommended vesting period. What happens if you need money now? A HECM Term payment can bridge your income gap.

(5) Gap Funding for Healthcare: While Medicare covers many medical expenses, it may not cover everything. HECM monthly payments can help bridge the gap between what Medicare covers and what it does not. It can also fill in if you must leave your job early and need funding until healthcare kicks in at age 65.

(6) Self-Funding for Extended Care: Monthly payments can be set up to cover the out-of-pocket expenses of extended care for as long as possible. When the care is no longer needed, the payments can be stopped and the remaining funds (if any) returned back to the line of credit where they are allowed to grow.

(7) Tax Bracket Management: Proceeds from a reverse mortgage are tax-free, so tapping into reverse mortgage dollars can decrease the amount a retiree needs to withdraw from taxable accounts. This simple action not only helps to reduce standard taxation but could also reduce the amount of Social Security benefits subject to income taxes. For higher-income retirees, tax-free reverse mortgage payments can reduce their modified adjusted gross income, which lowers the risk of higher monthly Medicare premiums.

(8) Premium Replacement Dollars: There are many cases in retirement where we may need to strategically replace income we have allocated for some other expense. This often happens with insurances. The reverse mortgage monthly payments can be used to fund everyday living expenses so that retirement income can be allocated to premium payments.

Having the ability to use your Housing Wealth to strategically create monthly income when needed changes the conversation. I think it's fair to say that a whole new set of planning possibilities may be open to you (not to mention the activities and travel you could pursue).

9

The HECM Replacement Strategy

What would retirement be like if you didn't have to make a monthly loan payment?

According to the Consumer Finance Protection Bureau, more people are carrying mortgage debt into their retirement years with some studies estimating that 50-68 percent of new retirees will have some sort of loan payment. For those 75 and older, housing expenses (mortgages, property taxes, insurance, utilities, home maintenance, and the like) account for a whopping 43 percent of their monthly spending.

When you combine a house payment with low savings and longer life expectancy, the prospect of eliminating a monthly mortgage payment and creating cash flow could be a huge relief.

Let's look at recent retirees, Pierce and Linda (65), to see how the reverse mortgage can help.

Pierce and Linda Eliminate Their Mortgage Payments

- **$400,000 home value**
- **$150,000 mortgage**
- **$800 a month for the next 25 years**

Pierce and Linda can make their payment each month, but don't want the responsibility of paying a mortgage until they are 90 years old.

They schedule an appointment to meet with their financial advisor. As he was reviewing their retirement goals and desires, assets and current budget, he asked them a question, **"Pierce, Linda, what would life be like if you didn't have to make a monthly mortgage payment?"**

They replied, "That would be great! We could do more things we enjoy without feeling guilty or concerned and even sleep a little better at night knowing we are not carrying this loan payment for the next 25 years."

After some more discussion, their advisor described how a reverse mortgage might replace their existing mortgage and eliminate their payments. He gave them some educational materials and encouraged them to investigate it more on their own.

What They Discovered

Pierce and Linda learned that a reverse mortgage must be a first mortgage, so any proceeds from the loan would need to be enough to pay off their existing mortgage(s) and home equity loan(s).

- They went to an online calculator **www.HousingWealth Calculator.com** and found out that they would be eligible for around $175,000 (based on the age of the youngest borrower, value of the home, and current interest rate).
- This was enough to pay off their existing $150,000 mortgage balance.
- This strategy would help them achieve two immediate benefits: (1) they would no longer have a mandatory loan payment of $800 and (2) they would have access to a $25,000 growing line of credit in a reserve fund.

"This is perfect," they thought. "The elimination of our mortgage payment and a fund for emergencies is just what the doctor ordered."

The CEO Is No Different from Pierce and Linda

Recall the retired CEO who was looking into a reverse mortgage. Why was he considering it?

He had a 4.5 million-dollar home, but over the years he had borrowed against it and now owed more than 2-million dollars. He was paying more than $20,000 a month just in principal and interest. Although he had 5-million dollars in investments and, conceivably, could have covered his monthly payment from those funds, his desire was the peace of mind that comes from not having to pay $240,000 a year in loan payments.

In that regard, he wasn't that different from many of us. Whether you're paying $20,000; $2,000; or $700 a month, you'd probably prefer not to have a mandatory monthly loan payment.

With the CEO's individual circumstances in mind, I suggested he consider an alternative to the reverse mortgage that better fit his needs. In the end, he sold his home, paid off the mortgage, added the additional dollars back to his savings and rented a summer home at the beach each year.

8 Benefits of Eliminating a Mandatory Loan Payment

Here are some retirement enhancing benefits of eliminating a mandatory monthly loan payment.

(1) Retirement Savings Can Last Longer: Many retirees don't have enough in savings to provide the type of retirement they desire...for as long as they desire. Any improvement that helps their money last longer is ideal.

Let's return to Pierce and Linda's story. They have retirement savings of $300,000 of which they were taking about $2,000 a month. By obtaining a reverse mortgage, they experience tremendous positive benefits for their savings (outlined below).

Results Summary

	A Traditional Mortgage	B HECM - No Mortgage Payment
Starting amount	$300,000	$300,000
Years you wish to make withdrawals	30 years	30 years
Periodic withdrawal from savings	$2,000 per month	$1,200 per month
Rate of return	4% compounded annually	4% compounded annually
Total amount they will have withdrawn	$411,386	$432,386
Ending balance	Client ran out of money at year 17	$148,000 remaining at year 30

In **Column A**, we see that Pierce and Linda have $300,000 in savings (starting amount), growing at 4 percent. They need to withdraw $2,000 per month (periodic withdrawals from savings) to support their current lifestyle and monthly mortgage payments. In this simplified example, assuming nothing changes, they will run out of money in seventeen years and two months (ending balance).

However, as noted in **Column B**, when Pierce and Linda use the HECM to eliminate their existing mortgage payment, they reduce their draw by $800 - meaning they no longer need $2,000 a month, only $1,200. Instead of running out in 17 years, their savings will last all 30 years and they'll have nearly $150,000 remaining.

(2) More Money Each Month: Running out of savings may not be your primary concern. In that case, eliminating a mortgage payment means you can enjoy a few retirement extras every once in a while without real concern about breaking the budget.

(3) Grandchildren's Education: According to the student loan giant, Sallie Mae, as the cost of higher education continues to grow, the reliance on family contributions to keep up has increased as well. The cash flow liberated from the reverse mortgage could allow a grandparent to assist with a small monthly tuition stipend, a gift, or even a low or no-interest loan to their grandchildren. What a financial legacy to pass on!

(4) The Gift of Life Insurance: Providing a cash value life insurance policy for your grandchildren has some distinct advantages. The first is that it's very inexpensive to obtain! The policies usually provide a good, solid return, particularly in a low-interest-rate environment. Also, the plans usually offer tax-deferred growth, and many come with guaranteed returns - meaning your money will increase regardless of what happens in the financial market (as long as you keep making premium payments).

(5) Defer Social Security or Investment Portfolio Withdrawals: In an earlier chapter, we spoke about the power of deferring Social Security or tax-deferred savings when possible. Another way of deferring is to use your former mortgage payments to supplement all or part of your income while you wait.

(6) Replace Cost of Long-Term Care: The ability to cover potential, long-term care expenses by purchasing some sort of insurance policy is very wise, but retirees are often concerned about how they will cover the premiums if they meet the medical qualifications. The newly liberated income could fit perfectly in this situation.

(7) Replace Cost of Life Insurance Legacy: Purchasing life insurance for retirement planning purposes has been a cornerstone strategy for years. Younger retirees can especially benefit from this. The new policies now come with long-term benefits that can be built in.

(8) Protection for Policy Lapses: One of the real dangers of retirement is uncertainty. Sometimes, the premiums that fund your life insurance, long-term care insurance, or medical coverage plan are in danger of lapsing because of financial issues encountered in retirement or because the insurer has raised the rates. Eliminating your monthly mortgage payment and recovering those funds could help sustain your premium payments.

The list could go on and on. The freedom that comes from eliminating a mandatory monthly payment cannot be underestimated.

What Should I Do If a Reverse Mortgage Doesn't Entirely Eliminate My Mortgage?

Sometimes the proceeds from a reverse mortgage are not enough to pay off the existing mortgage obligations (which you know is a requirement). Many retirees are tempted to dismiss the reverse mortgage at this point, but that could be an opportunity lost.

Let's consider Mary's scenario. She is 67 with a $450,000 home and a $200,000 mortgage balance; her monthly payment is $2,000 a month.

The reverse mortgage makes $175,000 available, but her existing mortgage debt totals $200,000. She has a shortfall of $25,000 and four options to consider.

HECM Benefit	$175,000
Total Loan Balances	$200,000
Shortfall to Close	$25,000
Monthly Principal/Interest Payments	$2,000

Hope for a better appraisal value. Mary could choose to pursue the HECM and hope that her home's value comes in higher - eliminating any potential shortfall. With the current online tools available to consumers, I have found that most estimates are very close to the actual appraised value. Hoping for a better appraisal is usually not the best course of action.

Wait and continue paying down the current mortgage. Mary could wait a few years and then revisit the reverse mortgage. The hope would be that her loan balance would be less, and her home's value would be more. This strategy depends on the assumption that her house will be worth more and that the HECM program and interest rates will remain about the same. Sometimes, this is the only option a person has, but fortunately for Mary, she has a few other considerations.

Consider moving. If Mary is open to moving, she could sell her current home, pay off the mortgage, and then use the remaining proceeds to rent, move to a smaller home and pay cash, or use the HECM for Purchase strategy to rightsize into her next, last, and best retirement home (see chapter on HECM for Purchase).

Pull the additional dollars needed from savings. Lastly, Mary has $300,000 in her investment account, money in cash equivalents, a small annuity she isn't drawing from, and $50,000 of cash value in life insurance. She could choose to draw the $25,000 from one of those accounts and combine it with the HECM proceeds to pay off her current mortgage.

Investments	$300,000
Cash/CD/Money Market	$40,000
Existing Annuities	$50,000
Cash Value Life Insurance	$50,000

When Does It Make Sense to Pull from Savings?

Of the four options, Mary chose to bring the extra $25,000 from her CD's. She is not alone; I have found several clients happy to bring upwards of $100,000 to the table to get rid of their mandatory mortgage payments.

When does it make sense to do this? The answer lies mainly in how important it is to your retirement savings, lifestyle, and happiness to be free of the monthly mortgage payment. Is your monthly loan payment:

- √ Causing significant emotional concern and worry?
- √ Prematurely draining retirement savings?
- √ Preventing funds from being used for other resources?
- √ Forcing you to prematurely pull from an annuity?
- √ Keeping you from delaying Social Security?
- √ Inducing high credit card debt?

What you may discover is that drawing from savings to rid yourself of the burden of having a monthly loan payment is well worth it.

10

The HECM Exchange Strategy

There are only a few, new concepts in retirement planning that people would consider truly revolutionary. The strategy we will explore in this chapter is one of them. Perhaps you skimmed over the previous chapter because you don't have a monthly loan payment, or maybe the monthly payment you do have isn't really a burden. If that is true for you, this may be just the chapter you've been waiting for!

Maximize the "What If" Fund

David and Karen are preparing to retire. Both are in good health and believe they will live a long time. They eat right, exercise, and have saved modestly well for retirement.

- **$400,000 Home Value**
- **$100,000 Mortgage**
- **$1,000/Month Payment for 13 years**

Making a mortgage payment each month is not a hardship and they are comfortable that their current savings and budget are sufficient.

Their primary concerns are the projected expenses associated with health and long-term care, access to money for unexpected expenses, and the freedom to enjoy a retirement luxury every so often without guilt or concern.

David and Karen visited Cindy, their advisor, and shared their concerns. After listening, Cindy shared that she had just completed a Certificate Course in Housing Wealth Applications (CHWA) and would like to show them a strategy she had just seen. They agreed, and Cindy presented an idea that did not seem to make sense at first: **establish a reverse mortgage AND continue making monthly payments, except pay the reverse mortgage company instead!**

Here's how the conversation went:

Cindy: David and Karen, what would retirement be like if you didn't have to make a monthly mortgage payment?

David and Karen: It would be about the same. The payments aren't a burden to us; we're pretty comfortable.

Cindy: Great, let me make sure I understand. You have been paying your mortgage company $1,000 a month for the last seventeen years and you're financially comfortable continuing those payments?

David and Karen: Yes.

Cindy: So, in that time, you've paid them over $200,000. Let me ask you a question. If you were to call them right now and ask them to send you a check for $80,000 because you had a need, would they send it?

David and Karen: No, they would ask us to apply for a new loan, pull our credit and current debt, have us produce income documents and get approved, etc.

Cindy: Why wouldn't they give you access to the money you've paid over the years, especially if you had a pressing need?

David and Karen: I don't know. That's just the way the system works!

Cindy: How likely is it that you may need access to additional retirement dollars in the future?

David and Karen: I would say fairly likely, especially if we live long enough.

Cindy: What type of things would you need money for in the future?

David and Karen: Increasing taxes, healthcare, home repairs, unexpected expenses, loss of savings, helping children, a dream vacation, you name it.

Cindy: If there was a way you could take the mortgage payments you are already making and create an $850,000 reserve for healthcare and the other concerns you mentioned, would you want me to tell you about it?

David and Karen: Absolutely, but what do you mean?

Cindy: Since you are comfortable making payments, I don't want you to stop. I want you to continue making the same $1,000 payment on the same day and for roughly the same period of time, your current mortgage payments would have lasted. The only change I want you to make is WHO you make the payment to.

David and Karen were intrigued by the concept of keeping their existing payment and reducing their loan balance, while at the same time creating a reserve for expenses that could occur later in retirement.

Cindy sent them home with some educational material and asked them to speak with a HECM professional for more insight.

Understanding the HECM Exchange

After meeting with a housing wealth specialist and receiving HUD counseling, David and Karen proceeded to put this strategy in place.

The first step was to complete a standard HECM. Based on Karen's age (65), their $400,000 home value and the current interest rate, the reverse mortgage made $159,600 available.

As a requirement of the loan, their existing mortgage balance of $100,000 was paid off in full, leaving them with a $59,600 growing line of credit.

Home Value	$400,000
Reverse Mortgage Proceeds	$159,600
Existing Mortgage Balance	$100,000
Available HECM Line of Credit	$59,600

What Happens When They Make a Payment?

After David and Karen establish the HECM, the next step is to simply CONTINUE making a monthly payment of $1,000 - the same amount they were paying before, but they are now making payments to the reverse mortgage lender! When they make this payment on their reverse mortgage, two things happen simultaneously:

Their Outstanding Loan Balance Decreases

The top line represents their increasing home value. The middle line represents their available HECM Line of Credit, and the bottom line represents their outstanding balance.

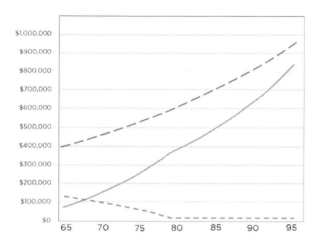

Their Available Line of Credit Dramatically Increases

Year	A	B
	Line of Credit No Voluntary Payments	Line of Credit with $12,000/yr Payment
0	$59,600	$59,600
5	$77,446	$144,257
10	$100,636	$254,262
15	$130,770	$389,657
20	$169,926	$506,358
25	$220,808	$657,958
30	$286,925	$854,997

The power of this strategy is that it takes the monthly mortgage payments David and Karen would have been paying anyway and uses them to reduce the outstanding balance of the HECM, while simultaneously adding funds to the available and growing line of credit for tax-free access in the future.

Notice how large the line of credit (Column B) grows when they are making a monthly payment!

Were David and Karen's primary concerns addressed by this strategy?

√ Since David and Karen were comfortable making a $1,000/ month payment, they voluntarily continued, and by year fifteen, their balance was nearing $0. (Note that they must leave at least a $100 balance, so the lender does not close the loan.)

√ At year 15 their accessible line of credit was nearly $400,000 versus $131,000 had they not made any voluntary payments.

√ By age 85 (the average age most people need some sort of extended care), Karen no longer needed to worry. She now has a back-up plan that exceeds $500,000 and they also have peace of mind should any other spending shock surprise them.

By using this reverse mortgage strategy, David and Karen have payment freedom and flexibility. Best of all, this strategy didn't require them to change anything except who they were now sending their monthly payment to.

If you are retired and comfortable making a monthly loan payment, then the HECM Exchange strategy certainly makes sense for your situation.

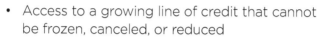

WHY WOULD A RETIREE CONTINUE TO MAKE A MANDATORY MONTHLY MORTGAGE PAYMENT WHEN THEY COULD EXCHANGE IT FOR A VOLUNTARY ONE AND GET MORE BENEFITS?

- Voluntary payments vs. mandatory
- Loan balance decreases with each payment
- Access to a growing line of credit that cannot be frozen, canceled, or reduced

Sometimes, however, as wonderful as this strategy can be, the house you currently live in may not be the best option for a sustainable retirement. When this happens, an entirely new type of reverse mortgage might be the ticket. We will talk about this in our final foundation.

11

The HECM for Purchase Strategy

If you could increase your cash flow, reduce your expenses, and add new money back into your retirement savings, but it involved moving to your next, last, and best home; would you want to know about it? Our final HECM Foundation is focused on helping retirees do just that.

We all love the history, memories, and familiarity of our homes, but the idea of an enhanced retirement in a new home - specifically purchased with our needs, desires, and income in mind – is very intriguing.

Bruce and Barbara Buy Their Retirement Dream Home

- Both are age 65, recently retired and in good health.
- $405,000 in savings | $24,000 initial withdrawal to maintain lifestyle
- $525,000 home (4,000 square feet)
- $100,000 mortgage |$1,000 monthly payment over next 12 years

Barbara's Retirement Concerns:

Barbara's primary concern is running out of savings. She has done some online calculating and believes that they have not saved enough to sustain their $24,000/year draw and adjust each year for inflation. She believes $16,000 a year is more sustainable.

Bruce's Retirement Concerns:

Bruce had planned to play more golf, maintain his club membership, and travel during the early years of retirement, but Barbara's worrying about the budget is taking the fun out of his golden years.

At dinner one evening, a realtor friend of theirs who had recently attended a workshop asked them:

"If you could increase your cash flow, reduce your expenses, and add new money back into your retirement savings, but it involved moving to your next, last, and best home; would you want to know about it?"

"Yes," they said as they began to consider what they just heard.

"More cash flow means more golf and travel without worry," thought Bruce.

"This means more money added to savings, so we can enjoy retirement and not worry about running out of money," thought Barbara.

"A newer house with less maintenance, lower taxes, and better amenities sounds great," said both of them.

A New Way to Buy Your Next Home

What Bruce and Barbara's friend was describing is a new type of reverse mortgage. In 2008, as part of the Housing and Economic Recovery Act (HERA), the U.S. Department of Housing authorized the HECM for Purchase (H4P). This reverse mortgage allows retirees to purchase a new home with the proceeds of the HECM financing a portion of the purchase price. A new home usually can be purchased with around a 50 to 60 percent downpayment and requires no monthly mortgage payments.

How Does it Work?

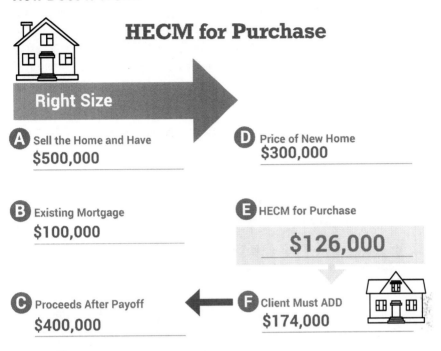

HECM for Purchase

Right Size

A Sell the Home and Have
$500,000

D Price of New Home
$300,000

B Existing Mortgage
$100,000

E HECM for Purchase
$126,000

C Proceeds After Payoff
$400,000

F Client Must ADD
$174,000

G Liberated Proceeds: $226,000

Notice the letters in the picture above as we outline the steps for this HECM for Purchase (H4P).

Step A: Bruce and Barbara sell their existing home, pay the realtor costs and transfer taxes, and have $500,000 left over.

Step B: They pay off their existing mortgage of $100,000. This frees them from the burden of the mandatory monthly mortgage payment.

Step C: They now have $400,000 left to put towards their next home. They can choose to move to a more expensive $500,000 home (upsize), to a similarly priced $400,000 home (same-size), or to a less expensive $300,000 home (downsize).

Step D: Bruce and Barbara choose to move to a $300,000 home. They have a few financing options:

(1) Pay Cash: They can use the $400,000 from the sale of their old house to pay cash for the new home and have $100,000 left over. The concern with this plan is locking up a majority of their proceeds in the new property. What happens if another housing correction happens and the home loses value? What happens if they cannot get the money out of the property when they need it? The prevailing wisdom in these days of economic uncertainty is to keep as much of their proceeds accessible as possible.

(2) Traditional Mortgage: They can make a smaller downpayment in cash and finance the remaining balance by taking out a traditional loan. They would have some proceeds left over in cash, but they would also have a new mandatory monthly mortgage payment, which was something neither of them wanted.

(3) HECM for Purchase (H4P): They can use the reverse mortgage (H4P) to finance a portion of the home's purchase.

Step E: Bruce and Barbara choose the HECM for Purchase. The H4P will finance around 40 to 50 percent based on their ages, the $300,000 home value and current interest rates. In their case, the H4P makes $126,000 (a little over 40% of the home's value) available to them.

Step F: They must add $174,000 of their own funds as the downpayment. (Here's the formula: Sale Price of Home - H4P Proceeds = $174,000)

Step G: After using $174,000 of the proceeds from the sale of their old house, they will have $226,000 left over.

Did the HECM for Purchase strategy do what their realtor friend said it could? Did it solve Bruce and Barb's retirement concerns?

Increase Cash Flow: When they sold their old home and paid off their mortgage, it eliminated their monthly mortgage payment of $1,000 a month. Now they have $1,000 a month in extra cash flow to do the things they want (golfing and traveling) without financial worry. This made Bruce happy.

Reduce Expenses: In addition to eliminating their monthly mortgage payment, they have moved from a $525,000, 4,000-square foot home to a newer, better built, more energy efficient, $300,000 home with 2,000-square feet. Newer appliances, less maintenance, and lower taxes will help keep their expenses down.

Add New Dollars Back into Savings: They were able to add $226,000 to their existing savings ($405,000) for a new total of $631,000. Now that they don't have a mortgage payment and have lowered their overall expenses, $631,000 is more than sufficient to sustain a comfortable lifestyle for all of their retirement. This made Barb happy.

How Does Moving to a Bigger House Work?

We have all seen the signs: "Homes from the Low $300's" or "Move Here from the mid $500's." These places look great with their club-houses, manicured yards, fitness centers, and swimming pools. For some, however, the question is: how can we afford to move to one of these communities, if our current home doesn't provide enough proceeds after we sell it?

Take Sam and his wife for example. They sold their home, received $400,000 in proceeds and wanted to buy a home that costs $600,000. They didn't want to pull the extra money from savings

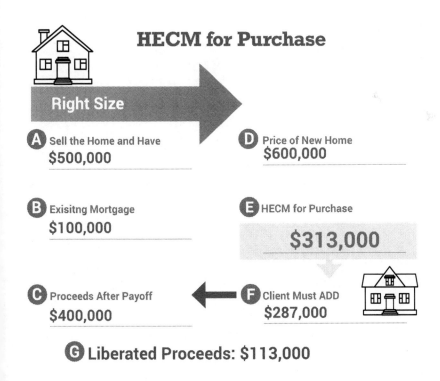

HECM for Purchase

Right Size

A Sell the Home and Have
$500,000

D Price of New Home
$600,000

B Exisitng Mortgage
$100,000

E HECM for Purchase
$313,000

C Proceeds After Payoff
$400,000

F Client Must ADD
$287,000

G Liberated Proceeds: $113,000

and absolutely did not want to take a traditional mortgage and make payment.

They chose to use the HECM for Purchase to finance a portion of their purchase price (Step E), they brought a $287,000 downpayment and had $113,000 leftover to add to savings.

The good news is that the H4P program works for nearly any home value. The following illustration shows different ages and home values. Just find the nearest age of the youngest borrower and note the value of the home you wish to buy.

Purchase $	Age of Youngest Borrower					
	62	65	70	75	80	85
$150,000	$96,267	$93,117	$88,017	$84,117	$77,967	$69,867
$200,000	$126,717	$122,517	$115,717	$110,517	$102317	$91,517
$250,000	$156,667	$151,417	$142,917	$136,417	$126,167	$112,667
$300,000	$186,617	$180,317	$170,117	$162,317	$150,017	$133,817
$350,000	$216,567	$209,217	$197,317	$188,217	$173,867	$154,967
$400,000	$247,517	$239,117	$225,517	$215,117	$198,717	$177,117
$450,000	$276,967	$267,517	$250,217	$240,517	$222,067	$197,767
$500,000	$306,417	$295,917	$278,917	$265,917	$245,417	$218,417
$550,000	$335,867	$324,317	$305,617	$291,317	$268,767	$239,067
$600,000	$365,317	$352,717	$332,317	$316,717	$292,117	$259,717
*Down Payment						

If you find yourself in a situation where you want the home of your retirement dreams or a home that allows you to add more savings, so you can have a better retirement, then the HECM for Purchase might be what you have been looking for.

In the next chapter, we will summarize the HECM Foundations by looking at how one couple combined several housing wealth strategies to create the retirement plan of their dreams.

12

Tying It All Together How One Couple Got Exactly What They Wanted

Remember the family discussion from an earlier chapter? The brave souls who mentioned a reverse mortgage at the family picnic? Let's explore their situation and see how a reverse mortgage might help them.

Jack and Diane

- ✓ Age 65/65
- ✓ Married for 40 years
- ✓ 3 children
- ✓ 7 grandchildren
- ✓ Lived in their home for last 25 years

Financial Summary

- ✓ $300,000 in savings 401K and an Investment Account
- ✓ $100,000 in CDs, Money Market and Cash (as a reserve)
- ✓ $450,000 home value
- ✓ $100,000 mortgage balance
- ✓ Paying $841 a month

Financial Concerns

- ✓ Longevity | Lifestyle | Liquidity
- ✓ Both are in relatively good health but are concerned that the cost of an extended care episode as they age could have a devastating impact on their finances.

✓ Jack retired, but Diane would like to work longer. However, her job is changing and her employer wants her to take early retirement or go to part-time.

Financial Goals

✓ Fixed, predictable **Revenue** to cover their retirement essentials.

✓ Better retirement **Returns** to cover their retirement enjoyment.

✓ An accessible **Reserve** for unexpected expenses or unplanned purchases.

Jack and Diane, like many of today's retirees, did not have anyone they considered their personal financial advisor or a written retirement plan. They had invested through their respective company retirement plans and put savings away themselves. By all standards, they had done fairly well.

They recently read a report that said retirees do better financially (and emotionally) in retirement when they seek the guidance of a professional advisor, so they asked for some recommendations and finally met with an advisor named Sharon.

Before their initial meeting, Sharon asked them to fill out a fact finder about their income, expenses, savings, retirement lifestyle desires, legacy goals, long-term care concerns, etc. When they met in person, she reviewed it with them. She also shared that her philosophy of creating optimized retirement income plans was rooted in her commitment to factor in all of her clients' available assets.

The 4 Buckets

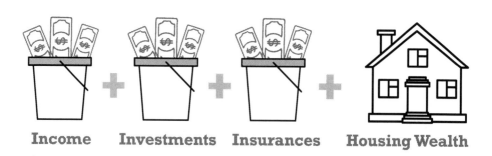

Income   Investments   Insurances   Housing Wealth

She explained the Income, Investment, Insurance, and Housing Wealth Buckets and asked if Jack and Diane had any objections to her exploring the items and strategies in each. Was anything off limits?

Jack and Diane said any viable strategy was okay with them but wanted to know why she was including reverse mortgages.

Sharon understood and handed them a statement of understanding, so they could read it together.

> "As an advisor, I have a responsibility to do what is in the best interest of my clients. Part of that responsibility means staying informed about current thoughts, trends, and legitimate resources that could have a positive or negative effect upon my ability to help my clients meet their retirement goals.
>
> For the last several years, the Home Equity Conversion Mortgage (HECM) also known as a reverse mortgage has grown in popularity, and recent research suggests that the strategic use of reverse mortgages may be helpful in positively impacting retirement outcomes.
>
> I believe that in order to engage in a thorough and comprehensive financial plan for my clients, the housing asset should not be ignored if certain, desired retirement outcomes are to be achieved.
>
> By no means do I suggest that a reverse mortgage is right for every client (far from it), but I do acknowledge the importance of the housing asset in the retirement planning conversation."

She went on to say that reverse mortgages are not an approved product of her firm; that she is not authorized to discuss rates, terms, fees, etc.; that she does not receive any compensation should they move forward; and that the loan proceeds cannot be invested in any financial products.

Jack and Diane were very pleased by the explanation and her commitment to not excluding any "treatment options."

As Sharon continued the review, she came to their monthly expenses and asked them a question, "What would retirement be like if you didn't have to make a monthly mortgage payment?"

Jack and Diane said they could continue to pay it but would be more comfortable if they didn't have to. This started a brainstorming session of all the ways their retirement could be different, if they didn't have to make a payment each month. The conversation led to Sharon showing them a **Customized Housing Wealth Illustration*** of a few simple strategies for incorporating a reverse mortgage to meet their financial goals. She also suggested that they view some educational videos online www.HousingWealthVideos.com. They proved to be quite a catalyst in helping create a retirement plan.

After more conversation about portfolio allocation, fixed income, life insurance, and legacy goals, Sharon sent Jack and Diane home with some educational resources. She asked them to do some reverse mortgage research for themselves and scheduled their next meeting in two weeks.

Steps to Financial Peace of Mind

Step 1: The first thing Jack and Diane did was go online to **www.HousingWealthCalculator.com** to get a ballpark figure of how much the reverse mortgage would make available - $170,850.

Step 2: From those proceeds, the reverse mortgage would pay off their existing mortgage of $100,000 and eliminate their mandatory monthly payments of $841. [HECM Replacement]

Step 3: It would also leave them with a growing line of credit of $70,850, which they also discovered could be converted to monthly payments at any time in the future. Having access to this money would fulfill their desire for liquidity and give them

Age	LOC Amount	Tenure Pmt	5 yr Term	10 yr Term
65	$70,850	$384	$1,351	$770
70	$93,799	$537	$1,789	$1,019
75	$124,182	$768	$2,368	$1,349
80	$164,407	$1,137	$3,135	$1,786
85	$217,660	$1,785	$4,151	$2,365
89	$272,438	$2,760	$5,195	$2,960

peace of mind to know it was at their fingertips. [HECM Line of Credit and Monthly Payment]

Step 4: Because they would have a $70,850 standby reserve that they could access at any time, they could feel comfortable enough to move the $100,000 reserve they had in low-producing accounts into the annuity they wanted, which would guarantee fixed, predictable income for life. Their retirement essentials would be covered.

Step 5: With their monthly essentials covered by the fixed income and their mandatory monthly mortgage payment eliminated, they realized they could take significantly less from their savings each month allowing them to last much longer.

Step 6: No longer having an $841 monthly mortgage payment, they realized they could use some of the dollars they had been spending each month to strengthen gaps in their retirement income plan. They decided to discuss with Sharon the purchase of a traditional long-term care insurance policy. It felt good to know that they would have access to care in the future, be able to protect their assets, and wouldn't be a burden on their loved ones.

Step 7: No longer having an $841 monthly mortgage payment, they realized they could look into buying life insurance for themselves and for their grandchildren or just keeping the money for enjoyment each month. They're thinking a two-week cruise would be a fun summer vacation.

They couldn't wait to share with Sharon some of the discoveries they had made and get her feedback.

Endless Possibilities

In the meeting, they described how Housing Wealth could work in coordination with their other assets to achieve the retirement goals.

+ Fixed, predictable **Revenue** to cover their retirement essentials.

+ Better retirement **Returns** to cover their retirement enjoyment.

+ An accessible **Reserve** for unexpected expenses or un-planned purchases.

By the end of the second meeting, Jack and Diane were so thrilled with Sharon's process and professionalism that they asked her to manage the rest of their $300,000 savings as well.

Jack and Diane are just one example of how the five Foundations (Line of Credit, Monthly Payment, Replacement, Exchange, and Purchase) can be mixed and matched to create all types of positive retirement outcomes.

*A Picture is Worth a Thousand Words

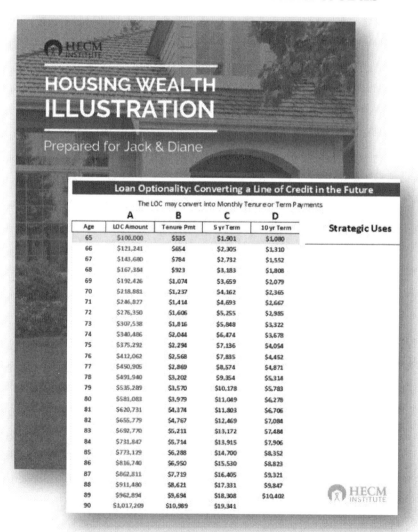

HOUSING WEALTH ILLUSTRATION

Prepared for Jack & Diane

Loan Optionality: Converting a Line of Credit in the Future				
The LOC may convert into Monthly Tenure or Term Payments				
	A	B	C	D
Age	LOC Amount	Tenure Pmt	5 yr Term	10 yr Term	Strategic Uses
65	$100,000	$535	$1,901	$1,080	
66	$121,241	$654	$2,305	$1,310	
67	$143,680	$784	$2,732	$1,552	
68	$167,384	$923	$3,183	$1,808	
69	$192,426	$1,074	$3,659	$2,079	
70	$218,881	$1,237	$4,162	$2,365	
71	$246,827	$1,414	$4,693	$2,667	
72	$276,350	$1,606	$5,255	$2,985	
73	$307,538	$1,816	$5,848	$3,322	
74	$340,486	$2,044	$6,474	$3,678	
75	$375,292	$2,294	$7,136	$4,054	
76	$412,062	$2,568	$7,835	$4,452	
77	$450,905	$2,869	$8,574	$4,871	
78	$491,940	$3,202	$9,354	$5,314	
79	$535,289	$3,570	$10,178	$5,783	
80	$581,083	$3,979	$11,049	$6,278	
81	$620,731	$4,374	$11,803	$6,706	
82	$655,779	$4,767	$12,469	$7,084	
83	$692,770	$5,211	$13,172	$7,484	
84	$731,847	$5,714	$13,915	$7,906	
85	$773,129	$6,288	$14,700	$8,352	
86	$816,740	$6,950	$15,530	$8,823	
87	$862,811	$7,719	$16,405	$9,321	
88	$911,480	$8,621	$17,331	$9,847	
89	$962,894	$9,694	$18,308	$10,402	
90	$1,017,209	$10,989	$19,341		

HECM INSTITUTE

Earlier I mentioned that Jack and Diane were shown a **Customized Housing Wealth Illustration** by their advisor. This is a very important resource when it comes to evaluating the impact of a reverse mortgage on your retirement outcomes because it's able to **highlight**:

- The estimated growth of the HECM Line of Credit
- The potential term and tenure payments options, if the line is converted at certain points in the future
- The potential growth and convertibility of the line credit AFTER an existing loan is paid off
- The impact of making a voluntary monthly loan payment to the HECM

As you consider if the new reverse mortgage could help you achieve (or maintain) the retirement you desire, please make sure to ask your advisor for a Customized Housing Wealth Illustration. You can also go to www.HousingWealthPartners.com, and we can direct you towards a professional who can provide one. Let's proceed on to the final step.

√ **Step 1:** Get the Basics: Myths and Misconception About How the Reverse Mortgage Works

√ **Step 2:** Learn the Foundational Strategies: Five Ways to Incorporate Reverse Mortgages

☐ **Step 3:** Evaluate If It's Right for You

SECTION 4:

HOW TO KNOW IF THE REVERSE MORTGAGE IS THE BEST CHOICE FOR YOU

13

Three Questions to Ask Before Applying for a Reverse Mortgage

I hope by this point you have seen that reverse mortgages can offer so much more than expected. The five foundations and their corresponding stories should have shed a lot of light on the power and versatility of including Housing Wealth in retirement planning.

Now we turn our attention to the three questions that need to be answered before deciding if the reverse mortgage is the best option for your situation.

Question 1: What Does Cost?

Everyone knows that financial products, services, and strategies all have a cost associated with them. Whether you buy a life or long-term care insurance policy, annuity, mutual fund, CD or received a written plan from an advisor, it all has a cost. Reverse mortgages are no different.

The closing costs of a reverse mortgage have varied from a few hundred dollars to several thousands. Economic variables, public policy, as well as periodic program changes made by the government can cause pricing vacillations. Therefore, standard HECM pricing will continue to ebb and flow.

However, here are the three standard acquisition cost categories for the HECM reverse mortgage program that have remained consistent.

FHA Mortgage Insurance Premiums. This required insurance is purchased by the borrower and goes to the Federal Housing Administration. It guarantees that the borrower's total debt repayment will never be greater than the value of the home at the time of repayment. It also ensures that neither the borrower, their heirs, nor their estate will have any personal liability for repayment of the loan. Finally, it guarantees that the borrower will receive the promised loan advances and will not have to repay the loan for as long as they live in the home and meet the loan requirements.

Loan Origination Fee. The lender is permitted to charge a fee to cover their costs for setting up the loan. The maximum amount that can be charged is between $1,750 and $6,000, depending on home value.

Third-Party Fees. This includes costs charged by third-party vendors associated with transacting and closing the loan such as title insurance, appraisal, credit report, settlement fee, endorsements, counseling, flood/tax certificate, and a notary.

Below is a chart outlining the standard acquisition costs for a HECM at time of writing.

How Are the Closing Costs Typically Paid?

Like most home equity loans and mortgages, the closing costs of a HECM are financed into the loan. The only out-of-pocket expenses are for the appraisal and any fee the FHA counselor may charge. The total amount is usually between $300 - $495, and for most people, this makes all the difference in the world.

HECM Acquisition Costs

Description/Purpose	Home Values		
	$200,000	$400,000	$600,000
✓ Mortgage Insurance Premium	$4,000	$8,000	$12,000
✓ Lender Origination	$4,000	$6,000	$6,000
✓ Third-Party Charges	$1,000	$2,000	$3,000
	$9,000	$16,000	$21,000

I once asked a client how much their home's value had increased since they bought it 35 years ago. They told me the price had increased 5x! They bought it for $70,000 and now it's worth more than $350,000. I then asked them if it would be alright for their house to share some of the growth it experienced over the last 35 years and cover the costs of a getting reverse mortgage.

They certainly got the point. The house will make the "premium payments" for the equity insurance so that their personal cash flow doesn't have to!

Question 2: What Will It Accomplish?

Sometimes the fact that the house pays the closing costs is still not enough, and a retiree will still say, "Reverse mortgages are expensive."

"Compared to what?" is my usual response. I say this because we first need to know what the product is and does before we can assess its "value." Simply stated: it's very hard to determine the true cost of a financial strategy until you know the seriousness of the problem it's solving.

A reverse mortgage strategy must accomplish at least one of three things:

√ **Solve a Problem**

√ **Insure a Risk**

√ **Fulfill a Desire**

Solving a Problem

If a HECM strategy is not solving a financial problem, then it may not be the right solution, and the costs of acquisition may not be justified. However, if it does solve the problem then the "costs" may not be relevant. The following story may help me explain it better.

The University of Kentucky basketball program had gotten a reputation for recruiting superstar high school players who spent one year in college and

then declared for the NBA draft. Kentucky had done it yet again: they recruited a young man named Steve who was the best basketball player the university had EVER seen.

Right before NCAA finals, Steve noticed his right eye was a little blurry in the mornings. A few days later, both eyes were blurry. It wasn't too bad - just a nuisance - but before the week's end, he was really struggling to see and suspected something was seriously wrong.

He told his coaches and team doctors. They called in his parents and flew him to the best vision specialist in the country.

After a few hours and several tests, the results came in. "Steve, we have good news and bad news," said the doctor.

"What is the bad news, doc?"

"The bad news," said the doctor, "is you have a very rare condition that is causing accelerated blindness in both eyes. Unfortunately, in two to three weeks, you will be totally and irreversibly blind."

Alarmed and filled with tears, his mother asked, "What could possibly be the good news?"

The doctor replied, "Oh, the good news is that it's 100 percent treatable with a 99.9 percent success rate because we caught it early. Recovery should last about two weeks, and you won't have to worry about this issue ever coming back again."

Huge relief swept over the room. There were tears of joy, hugs and a sigh of relief from Steve's agent.

Then, from the corner, the voice of his father said, "Can I ask a question?"

"Of course," the doctor replied.

"How much will this cost?"

Stunned with disbelief, the doctor answered, "His eyesight."

The father's question, given the circumstances, was absurd because **the price of the procedure was not the same as the cost to the patient.**

The "cost" was the irreversible loss of his vision in both eyes and the subsequent financial loss of not playing in the NBA.

Although this story is fictional, the lesson it teaches is important. When it comes to retirement, security, and peace of mind, the real question regarding reverse mortgages is: what financial problem does it solve? Or better stated: what is the cost of NOT doing the reverse mortgage?

Always remember, the cost of a reverse mortgage is different from its price!

What is the cost of <u>NOT</u> doing the reverse mortgage?

Insuring a Risk

Most people do not purchase insurance because they want to use it; they purchase it because they don't want to bear the personal financial responsibility if something were to happen.

Think about it this way: What is the consequence of not having homeowners insurance when something serious happens? Simple: you carry the sole risk of paying the cost of damage. It's called Liability Transfer Risk. If you are not insuring the risk, then you are assuming it!

There are times in life when we make a choice to shoulder an expense to insure against something that may or may not happen in the future:

√ When the doctor said the growth was not cancerous but could develop into something later in life and suggests that you do surgery and/or a treatment protocol just to be safe.

√ When the car dealer says that you might want to consider the extended warranty just in case.

√ When your advisor says you should have six to twenty-four months of cash reserve to cover expenses and lifestyle should you end up out of work.

We are all accustomed to making daily decisions about the risks of life and whether we want to bear the financial responsibility if something goes sideways. If we don't want to bear it, we simply choose to pay for insurance ahead of time just in case something goes wrong.

Does your retirement income need insuring? Are you willing to bear the financial responsibility if your retirement outcomes don't go as expected? Are you willing to continue in retirement without a viable back-up plan to insure those risks?

As you've seen throughout the book, the reverse mortgage can act as a type of insurance policy to protect your savings from many of the 18-retirement income risks.

Fulfilling a Desire

Sometimes retirement is going great, and there are no worries about running out of savings or long-term care. All insurances and contingencies are in place. This is typically when it is appropriate to use the reverse mortgage to fulfill a desire: the vacation you've always wanted or the car with all the upgrades. The list is endless.

Over my 20 years, I have seen retirees choose a luxury type purchase over a strong retirement plan. It's easy to do, and we have all made similar choices. In retirement, however, there are no "do-overs." The choices you make have a greater impact. I strongly encourage those who want to make a more expensive purchase with reverse mortgage proceeds to make sure their other concerns and risks are covered first.

We've asked what a reverse mortgage costs and what it accomplishes. Now there's one question left to answer.

Question 3: What Alternative Works Better?

I hope I've been clear that I do not believe a reverse mortgage is always the best option. It must be weighed against other viable alternatives to discover which better solves the problem, insures the risk or fulfills the desire. Here are the top eight alternatives I have found over the last 20 years.

> **(1) Sell and Move:** This is always my first suggested consideration because it is often the most effective alternative for a successful retirement.

(2) Cash in Other Resources: Sometimes clients have savings, investments, or permanent life insurance from which they're willing to draw, or they may consider selling or borrowing on a second home to solve the financial challenge. You must weigh the benefits of using all or some of these other resources to meet the need.

(3) Borrow Money from Family: I have found that most children are willing to help their parents, but often are not prepared to provide the amount of money their parents may need for an extended retirement. Furthermore, my clients have been uncomfortable asking their children for this type of help. Would you be comfortable having your children assist you with your retirement income needs?

(4) Refinance: Consider taking out a home equity loan and making payments or refinancing an existing one into a lower payment. This is a good choice for some, but for others, it does not solve the cash flow or savings-erosion problems. The difficulties may be lessened, but the ultimate problem may still persist.

(5) Find a Roommate: Renting out a spare room or finding a senior roommate can often be a good solution. It provides income and companionship when it works well.

(6) Research Local Programs: Some retirees may be eligible for local programs that provide essentials. Cash and food assistance, along with home repair or weatherization, are often available to clients who meet the income requirements.

(7) Go Back to Work: Retirees have mixed reactions to this. Some say they'd like to, but no one will hire them. Others say, "Not on your life." Most are somewhere in between. Regardless of their reaction, part-time work is often a great retirement income supplement.

(8) Do Nothing/Wait: Sometimes waiting or doing nothing is the most appropriate thing to do. My experience has taught me that in most cases, by the time the HECM conversation comes up, the situation has worsened. I will often ask, "If you don't make some changes, do you think things will get better or worse?"

Is there anything I have missed? Here's the point: if the reverse mortgage is not the absolute best alternative to help you solve a financial problem, insure a potential risk or fulfill a desire, then you should not get one! It's just that simple.

However, if the reverse mortgage is the best alternative, then you should have 100% confidence in moving forward. You've looked at the issues head-on, been honest, and examined all the alternatives.

The following chapter will give you a road map for the next steps.

14

Next Steps – The Road Map

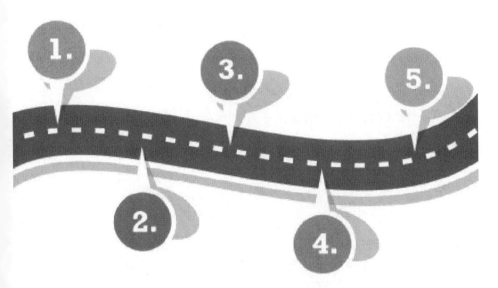

So, you believe that the reverse mortgage might be the right strategy for your retirement. What steps should you take? What things should you expect as you move forward?

Step 1: Review the Five Major Concerns of Retirement

Recall your top two retirement concerns and check them off here.

☐ **Longevity:** On a scale of 1 to 10, how much does the thought of running out of savings in retirement trouble you?

☐ **Lifestyle:** On a scale of 1 to 10, how disappointed would you be if you had to adjust your standard of living to make your savings last?

☐ **Liquidity:** On a scale of 1 to 10, how prepared are you for unexpected spending shocks in retirement?

- ☐ **Legacy:** On a scale of 1 to 10, how important is it to you to leave a financial legacy?

- ☐ **Long Term Care:** On a scale of 1 to 10, how prepared would you be if you had to access an additional $300,000 for health care-related costs?

Step 2: Determine Which Housing Wealth Strategy (or Strategies) Works Best for You

- ☐ **HECM Line of Credit:** An accessible and growing reserve

- ☐ **HECM Monthly Payments:** Term and Tenure

- ☐ **HECM Replacement:** Eliminate an existing mortgage

- ☐ **HECM Exchange:** Switch partners and make voluntary payments

- ☐ **HECM for Purchase:** Moving to next, last and best home for retirement enjoyment

Step 3: Use a Calculator to Get a Ballpark Estimate of Benefits

Calculate your potential benefit
www.HousingWealthCalculator.com

Step 4: Speak with Your Advisor or Find One Who Understands Housing Wealth

Studies have proven that retirees experience better retirement outcomes and peace of mind when they have a financial advisor and written financial plan. Throughout this book, we have absolutely encouraged you to consider meeting with one.

Step 5: Partner with the Right Reverse Mortgage Professional

For the last 20 years, I have been involved with HECMs and I can certainly tell you that all lenders are not the same. The product itself does not change, but the skill, knowledge, and application know-how of the reverse mortgage loan originator does. I recommend finding a lending partner who is:

+ Skilled and specialized in reverse mortgages.
+ Retirement-income focused
+ Housing-wealth certified

You can go to **www.HousingWealthPartners.com** to find some guidance.

 ## Step 6: The HECM Process - What to Expect

Once you select a Housing Wealth specialist, there a just a few simple steps to take you from start to finish.

Suitability Assessment: The specialist will review your concerns, determine your best strategy and calculate an estimate of proceeds.

Reverse Mortgage Counseling: You will then be directed to speak with a reverse mortgage counselor. This is a government requirement for all borrowers and usually takes 60-90 minutes. Most counseling is done by telephone. The counselor's job is to make sure you understand the program as well as other options and alternatives. At the end of the session, they will issue you a certificate of counseling.

Loan Application: After counseling, the lender will prepare a mortgage application package for you to sign and date.

Processing and Underwriting: Once the loan is submitted, the lender will order the appraisal and other services to determine the final value. They will look at your income, credit, and property tax payment history to make sure you are a suitable candidate for the program. The entire loan process varies, but you should typically anticipate anywhere between 4-8 weeks under normal circumstances.

Settlement/Loan Closing: Final documents will be signed.

Servicing: The organization that will send you statements, answer your questions and make disbursements from the line credit is called the servicer. They are usually specialty companies approved by the government. Sometimes the lender will service their own loan, but in recent times, this has been delegated to specialty firms.

Pretty straightforward right?

The road map gives you the comfort of knowing where you are going and provides the landmarks to look for along the way.

Online Resources at a Glance

- www.HousingWealthCalculator.com
- www.HousingWealthVideos.com
- www.HousingWealthPartners.com
- www.HousingWealth.net

Congratulations, you made it to the end. You have looked at the retirement landscape and its challenges. You have investigated the basics of the reverse mortgage program, explored the five foundations, and asked the questions needing answering before going forward.

√ **Step 1:** Get the Basics: Myths and Misconception About How the Reverse Mortgage Works

√ **Step 2:** Learn the Foundational Strategies: Five Ways to Incorporate Reverse Mortgages

√ **Step 3:** Evaluate If It's Right for You

SECTION 5:

ADDITIONAL AND ADVANCED STRATEGIES

This last section will cover a few advanced strategies for incorporating reverse mortgages in your retirement income plans. They're built on the five HECM Foundations we covered and designed to be a deeper dive, but very approachable; by the end, you should be able to explain the concepts on the back of a napkin.

15

Three Savvy Ways to Survive Market Volatility

The market goes up; the market goes down. The television analyst says we're in for a prolonged season of increasing gains, while a leading financial journal says we are now entering a time where market losses will be the norm versus the exception. Volatility!

The idea of volatility, another market correction or a prolonged down market is scary for retirees. Unlike younger workers who can ride out the market and let their accounts recover, retirees are actively taking money from their investment accounts. It's a very different picture - one that could be devastating to their retirement.

In this chapter, I will share three housing wealth strategies designed to help you weather the storm and come out on the other side better than you could have imagined.

Volatility and Average Rate of Return

We have all heard a report where the average rate of return on an investment was such and such. All this means is that the net total of the investment returns (positive and negative) was divided by the number of years in the market to give us an average rate of return. However, this does not tell the entire story.

For example, look at the next two charts on the following pages. They show a person retiring with $1,000,000 in their investment account over an 18-year period.

In **Chart 1** the market returns are positive during the early years and then have mainly negative returns towards the end. The ending portfolio balance is $2,095,393 and the average rate of return is 6.1%.

Age	Balance	S &P Returns	Yearly Withdrawal	Balance	Year
62	$1,000,000	12.0%	$0	$1,119,600	2000
63	$1,119,600	1.4%	$0	$1,134,827	2001
64	$1,134,827	13.5%	$0	$1,288,255	2002
65	$1,288,255	32.2%	$0	$1,702,429	2003
66	$1,702,429	15.9%	$0	$1,972,945	2004
67	$1,972,945	2.1%	$0	$2,014,377	2005
68	$2,014,377	14.8%	$0	$2,312,908	2006
69	$2,312,908	25.9%	$0	$2,912,876	2007
70	$2,912,876	-36.6%	$0	$1,848,220	2008
71	$1,848,220	5.5%	$0	$1,949,502	2009
72	$1,949,502	15.6%	$0	$2,253,819	2010
73	$2,253,819	4.8%	$0	$2,362,679	2011
74	$2,362,679	10.7%	$0	$2,616,431	2012
75	$2,616,431	28.4%	$0	$3,358,450	2013
76	$3,358,450	-22.1%	$0	$2,616,233	2014
77	$2,616,233	-11.9%	$0	$2,305,163	2015
78	$2,305,163	-9.1%	$0	$2,095,393	2016

Age	Portfolio Balance	S &P Returns	Balance	Yearly Withdrawal	End of Year Balance	Year
62	$1,000,000	-9.1%	$909,000	$0	$909,000	2000
63	$909,000	-11.9%	$800,920	$0	$800,920	2001
64	$800,920	-22.1%	$623,917	$0	$623,917	2002
65	$623,917	28.4%	$800,859	$0	$800,859	2003
66	$800,859	10.7%	$886,872	$0	$886,872	2004
67	$886,872	4.8%	$929,708	$0	$929,708	2005
68	$929,708	15.6%	$1,074,835	$0	$1,074,835	2006
69	$1,074,835	5.5%	$1,133,736	$0	$1,133,736	2007
70	$1,133,736	-36.6%	$719,355	$0	$719,355	2008
71	$719,355	25.9%	$905,956	$0	$905,956	2009
72	$905,956	14.8%	$1,040,219	$0	$1,040,219	2010
73	$1,040,219	2.1%	$1,062,063	$0	$1,062,063	2011
74	$1,062,063	15.9%	$1,230,825	$0	$1,230,825	2012
75	$1,230,825	32.2%	$1,626,536	$0	$1,626,536	2013
76	$1,626,536	13.5%	$1,846,443	$0	$1,846,443	2014
77	$1,846,443	1.4%	$1,871,555	$0	$1,871,555	2015
78	$1,871,555	12.0%	$2,095,393	$0	$2,095,393	2016

Chart 2 flips the returns, so that the negative years come early and the positive returns later. Notice that after 18 years, the account balances are exactly the same: $2,095,393 with a 6.1% rate of return!

How Bad Timing Affects Savings

But it's not realistic for the average person entering retirement to not make any withdrawals, is it? Let's see what happens when the retiree begins to draw money from their portfolio. We will use $50,000 draw each year over the same 18-year time frame.

Age	Portfolio Balance	S&P Returns	Balance	Yearly Withdrawal	End of Year Balance	Year
62	$1,000,000	12.0%	$1,119,600	$50,000	$1,069,600	2000
63	$1,069,600	1.4%	$1,084,147	$50,000	$1,034,147	2001
64	$1,034,147	13.5%	$1,173,963	$50,000	$1,123,963	2002
65	$1,123,963	32.2%	$1,485,317	$50,000	$1,435,317	2003
66	$1,435,317	15.9%	$1,663,389	$50,000	$1,613,389	2004
67	$1,613,389	2.1%	$1,647,270	$50,000	$1,597,270	2005
68	$1,597,270	14.8%	$1,833,986	$50,000	$1,783,986	2006
69	$1,783,986	25.9%	$2,246,752	$50,000	$2,196,752	2007
70	$2,196,752	-36.6%	$1,393,839	$50,000	$1,343,839	2008
71	$1,343,839	5.5%	$1,417,481	$50,000	$1,367,481	2009
72	$1,367,481	15.6%	$1,580,945	$50,000	$1,530,945	2010
73	$1,530,945	4.8%	$1,604,890	$50,000	$1,554,890	2011
74	$1,554,890	10.7%	$1,721,885	$50,000	$1,671,885	2012
75	$1,671,885	28.4%	$2,146,032	$50,000	$2,096,032	2013
76	$2,096,032	-22.1%	$1,632,809	$50,000	$1,582,809	2014
77	$1,582,809	-11.9%	$1,394,613	$50,000	$1,344,613	2015
78	$1,344,613	-9.1%	$1,222,253	$50,000	$1,172,253	2016

Chart 3 shows that if the retiree experiences early positive returns while drawing $50,000/year, they will have 1.1-million dollars remaining at the end of year 18. Not so bad, right?

Notice the difference; it's pretty dramatic! When the retiree experiences negative returns in the initial years of making withdrawals, they only have $359,987 (versus $1,172,253) remaining at the end of 18 years. Though both scenarios have the same average rate of return (6.1%), the impact of early negative returns is devastating. This is known as Sequence of Returns Risk. The bad news is that there's not much you can do about when you start taking from savings or what the market returns will be. That part is the luck of the draw.

What can retirees do to offset the negative consequences of market volatility and sequence risk? Continue reading to find out.

Age	Portfolio Balance	S &P Returns	Balance	Yearly Withdrawal	End of Year Balance	Year
62	$1,000,000	-9.1%	$909,000	$50,000	$859,000	2000
63	$859,000	-11.9%	$756,865	$50,000	$706,865	2001
64	$706,865	-22.1%	$550,648	$50,000	$500,648	2002
65	$500,648	28.4%	$642,631	$50,000	$592,631	2003
66	$592,631	10.7%	$656,280	$50,000	$606,280	2004
67	$606,280	4.8%	$635,563	$50,000	$585,563	2005
68	$585,563	15.6%	$676,970	$50,000	$626,970	2006
69	$626,970	5.5%	$661,328	$50,000	$611,328	2007
70	$611,328	-36.6%	$387,887	$50,000	$337,887	2008
71	$337,887	25.9%	$425,536	$50,000	$375,536	2009
72	$375,536	14.8%	$431,190	$50,000	$381,190	2010
73	$381,190	2.1%	$389,195	$50,000	$339,195	2011
74	$339,195	15.9%	$393,093	$50,000	$343,093	2012
75	$343,093	32.2%	$453,397	$50,000	$403,397	2013
76	$403,397	13.5%	$457,937	$50,000	$407,937	2014
77	$407,937	1.4%	$413,485	$50,000	$363,485	2015
78	$363,485	12.0%	$406,957	$50,000	$356,957	2016

Chart 4 paints a much different picture. It shows what happens when $50,000 is taken out each year with the returns flipped (like the 2nd chart), so that the negative years come early and the positive years later.

The Coordinated Strategy for Managing Risk

One way to address Sequence Risk is to convert some of the dollars you have in the market to less volatile vehicles. We will talk about that in the next chapter.

Another way to manage volatility is to reduce your spending in the year following a negative return until the portfolio recovers.

Chart 5 shows what would happen if you spent $0 in those years.

If you didn't take any money in the year following a poor return, you would have $902,158 eighteen years later (versus $356,957). That's nearly 2 times more! Problem solved!

Age	Portfolio Balance	S &P Returns	Balance	Yearly Withdrawal	End of Year Balance	Year
62	$1,000,000	-9.1%	$909,000	$50,000	$859,000	2000
63	$859,000	-11.9%	$756,865	$0	$756,865	2001
64	$756,865	-22.1%	$589,598	$0	$589,598	2002
65	$589,598	28.4%	$756,808	$0	$756,808	2003
66	$756,808	10.7%	$838,089	$50,000	$788,089	2004
67	$788,089	4.8%	$826,154	$50,000	$776,154	2005
68	$776,154	15.6%	$897,311	$50,000	$847,311	2006
69	$847,311	5.5%	$893,744	$50,000	$843,744	2007
70	$843,744	-36.6%	$535,355	$50,000	$485,355	2008
71	$485,355	25.9%	$611,257	$0	$611,257	2009
72	$611,257	14.8%	$701,845	$50,000	$651,845	2010
73	$651,845	2.1%	$665,534	$50,000	$615,534	2011
74	$615,534	15.9%	$713,342	$50,000	$663,342	2012
75	$663,342	32.2%	$876,606	$50,000	$826,606	2013
76	$826,606	13.5%	$938,363	$50,000	$888,363	2014
77	$888,363	1.4%	$900,445	$50,000	$850,445	2015
78	$850,445	12.0%	$952,158	$50,000	$902,158	2016

I suspect some of you are thinking, "If we spend $0 dollars in those years, how will we eat?!" Two popular strategies are:

- Use a cash reserve to supplement your income during the recovery period.
- Use cash from a permanent life insurance policy as a supplement.

There is a third way. Use your Housing Wealth! You can draw the money you need to live on from the reverse mortgage line of credit during the down years. Then you can replenish the line of credit when the portfolio recovers, or leave it as is. This is called the Coordinated Strategy.

It begins with establishing a reverse mortgage line of credit at the onset of retirement and then using some or all of it to cover income needs the year following a down year in the market.

Year	$200,000 ReLOC Value	$400,000 ReLOC Value	$600,000 ReLOC Value
0	$79,396	$162,796	$248,196
5	$103,118	$211,437	$322,353
10	$133,929	$274,611	$418,668
15	$173,945	$356,661	$543,760
20	$225,917	$463,227	$706,227
25	$309,167	$633,926	$966,472
30	$381,086	$781,391	$1,191,295

By doing this, you don't draw from the portfolio - locking in the losses - but rather draw from the reverse mortgage giving the portfolio time to recover.

Furthermore, because the proceeds of a reverse mortgage are not taxable, you can draw less than what you would need to draw from the portfolio to receive the same amount.

This just makes sense, doesn't it? For the out-of-pocket costs of $400 - $500 dollars, you can set up a ReLOC. It functions as a type of asset class, but one that is not tied to the market, so it is safe from negative fluctuations and principal erosion. You can use it as income after a negative portfolio year as well as keep it active for all the other applications we discussed earlier in the book. Having a plan B for market risk and volatility is smart planning.

Get More from Your Cash Reserve

As I mentioned earlier, having two to three years' worth of available, liquid funds to pull from when the market experiences a downturn is a common and recommended plan. What you will see is how the addition of a Housing Wealth conversation expands and even adds to this age-old strategy.

In July of 2012, Dr. Harold Evensky—known as the father of financial planning—delivered a keynote address at the Wharton School of the University of Pennsylvania. To everyone's surprise, he concluded his presentation by speaking about how reverse mortgages, particularly the line of credit and its financial planning implications, had really surprised him.

> "I see the reverse mortgage as a risk management tool—not as leverage, not as credit, not as cash flow. And unlike a home equity loan; it is non-cancelable, which is what happened during the grand recession. They got canceled. In this scenario, we go from a two-bucket approach to a three-bucket approach, where we can cut down that second bucket from two years to six months—and if we ever use that up—then we would tap into this reverse mortgage. The markets get better; we pay it back again." -Dr. Harold Evensky

This is brilliant in its simplicity.

Evensky's two buckets are the Investments Bucket and the Cash Reserves Bucket. By establishing a HECM line of credit as your reserve, you can move all, or most of, your emergency dollars from the Cash Bucket (low performing account) to the Investment Bucket (higher performing account) where they will attain higher returns.

If you need a cash infusion, you can draw from the HECM line of credit, and when markets rebound, pay it back (if you'd like). Evensky suggests that by doing this, you increase the likelihood

Repurposed Reserve Strategy

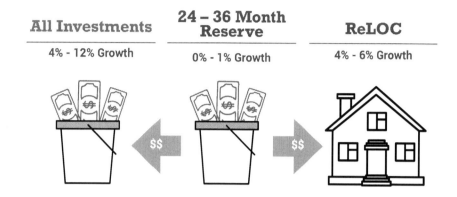

All Investments	24 – 36 Month Reserve	ReLOC
4% - 12% Growth	0% - 1% Growth	4% - 6% Growth

of success by repositioning low producing funds into more efficient vehicles without surrendering your back up plan for market volatility.

Setting a New Withdrawal Rate

We've talked about how to protect and boost your portfolio savings by having a standby reverse mortgage line of credit in place. One question remains: how much money can you NOW take out each year to reasonably make sure you will have enough to last for your lifetimes?

Let's look at Bill and Helen's story to learn more.

Bill and Helen are 65 and retiring at the end of the year. They have $500,000 saved in their IRA a 401k's and recently used an online retirement calculator to see how much they can begin drawing each year while ensuring the account lasts as long as their retirement does. Their calculator recommended following the "4% rule," which says they can initially draw out 4% of the $500,000, or $20,000 a year.

Bill and Helen were a little disappointed because they wanted a bit more than $20,000 a year to maintain their lifestyle. They shared their disappointment with their best friends, who suggested they speak with a retirement income specialist.

During their meeting with Kay, she asked them if it is okay for her to include their Housing Wealth in the conversation. Bill and Helen agreed, and the difference was eye-opening!

Kay showed that they could have an initial yearly withdrawal rate of $30,000 versus $20,000 by including Housing Wealth in the plan using a strategy called the "Rule of 30."

The Rule of 30

For years, a 4% initial withdrawal rate was the benchmark for how much you could draw from your portfolio. However, in 2017 Dr. Barry Sacks, Ph.D., suggested that the presence of Housing Wealth could enhance the initial withdrawal rate significantly.

He revealed his research in an article for the Journal of Financial Planning: *Integrating Home Equity and Retirement Savings through the 'Rule of 30*. In the article, Dr. Sacks outlined a formula that determines how much retirement income can be initially drawn from the portfolio of securities to sustain a thirty-year retirement.

His research describes a scenario where a retiree's principal sources of retirement income are from a portfolio of securities, they've accessed their home equity with a reverse mortgage line of credit, and they're using the coordinated draw strategy [discussed earlier in the chapter].

Here's How it Works

Dr. Sacks research says that you can add the value of your portfolio (at the outset of retirement) to the value of your home (also at the outset of retirement) and then divide the sum by thirty. This represents the initial withdrawal amount that can be taken in the first year of retirement. In the subsequent years, the withdrawal will be the same amount but adjusted for the previous year's inflation.

Let's compare how the online calculator and Kay arrived at different withdrawal rates.

> **Online Calculator:** The online calculator doesn't consider Housing Wealth and, therefore, doesn't recommend the Coordinated Draw Strategy. It simply used the standard 4% initial safe withdrawal rate. Therefore,

with a $500,000 portfolio, they will have an initial yearly income of $20,000.

Advisor Kay: Kay communicates the value of establishing a ReLOC and using the Coordinated Draw Strategy. Due to lowered risk, Bill and Helen can count both their housing wealth ($400,000) and existing portfolio ($500,000) to create a total wealth figure of $900,000. When Kay applies the "Sacks Rule of 30" and divides their total wealth of $900,000 by thirty, she obtains a new sustainable initial withdrawal rate of $30,000/year.

The Potential of Incorporating Housing Wealth

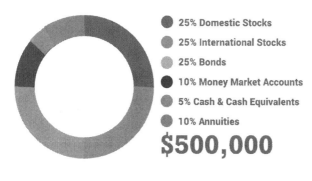

25% Domestic Stocks
25% International Stocks
25% Bonds
10% Money Market Accounts
5% Cash & Cash Equivalents
10% Annuities

$500,000

Initial Safe Withdrawal Rate
$20,000/yr.

$400,000

Initial Withdrawal Rate
$30,000/yr.

Volatility and market risk are part of investing, and managing those risks during the retirement years is essential. We've discovered that if you have money in the market during your retirement, then understanding the ability of a reverse mortgage line of credit to serve as a "shock absorber" for down markets, to repurpose cash reserves and to have a higher initial withdrawal rate could be some of the smartest retirement moves you could make - certainly something that should be part of your dialogue.

16

Strategies for the More Conservative Investor

Not every investor has the same level of risk tolerance. The last chapter was focused on retirees with a higher tolerance. Even though advisors know how to skillfully structure your retirement portfolio to mitigate many of the risks we discussed, some retirees find themselves wanting something more predictable, even if it may not grow or gain as much.

Over the years, I've become friends with two retirement income giants, Tom Hegna and Curtis Cloke. Both have popularized the use of fixed income vehicles (indexed, immediate, and deferred income annuities) in creating retirement income plans. Additionally, the American College of Financial Services and other thought leaders have been strong advocates for including guaranteed income in a modern retirement plan.

In Tom's book, *Paychecks and Playchecks,* as well as his popular PBS special, "Don't Worry, Retire Happy," he extols the virtue of having some predictable income. Curtis likes to use the phrase "Buy Income and Invest the Difference." Both Tom and Curtis' strategies are based on a very simple premise:

√ Convert a portion of your portfolio savings (Buy Income) into fixed income (Paychecks) to cover your retirement essentials. This often gives retirees peace of mind - knowing they have guaranteed income for life that isn't affected by market fluctuations.

√ Then repurpose your remaining portfolio savings (Invest the Difference) into a more aggressive allocation and use the returns to cover discretionary items like travel and family gifts (Playchecks). I call this guilt-free spending because it doesn't affect your daily essentials.

I must emphasize that the inclusion of these strategies is not meant to provide a blanket endorsement of their efficacy, but rather to display how the new reverse mortgage seamlessly incorporates into some of today's most popular planning concepts.

Creating Longevity When You're a Cautious Investor

Paula is 65, has never married, has $1-million invested, and lives in a $375,000 home with no mortgage. She enjoys good restaurants, theater, and travel and is the picture of good health.

Not a risk-taker, she is very reluctant to have all her savings in investments that could lose principal, but she also understands the need to keep some dollars in accounts that have higher growth potential and can keep pace with inflation.

She recently saw a PBS special called, "Don't Worry, Retire Happy," where the presenter was describing an "optimized" retirement. What he was saying made sense, so she decided to speak with her advisor and voice her concerns.

The Question Paula Was Asked

Paula felt her advisor was very knowledgeable, always had her best interests in mind, and seemed to keep current with strategies that were helpful. She was right!

When they met to review her concerns, he asked if Paula would be open to seeing how she could convert a portion of her assets to create the fixed income she wanted to cover living essentials, allocate the remaining investments to cover her discretionary expenses, and then use her housing wealth to create an inflation buffer and emergency reserve (that could also be turned into an income stream if needed).

Paula was intrigued and asked her advisor to continue explaining.

Step 1: Create Fixed Income

He asked Paula to calculate the amount of money she needs this year to cover her essentials. Paula believes she will need $40,000/year.

According to Tom Hegna and Curtis Cloke's strategy, Paula converted a portion of her investable assets ($1-million) and turned them into guaranteed fixed income for life (Paychecks).

Step 2: Reallocate Investments

Traditionally, most retirees' portfolios are divided between stocks and bonds (with stocks providing greater returns, but also greater risk). The younger you are, the more you can have allocated in stocks (perhaps 70/30) because you have the time to ride out market volatility. However, as you age and begin to withdraw money, the risk allocation shifts to 60/40, or even 50/50 because you have less time to absorb and recover from shocks.

Since Paula's income essentials are now covered and no longer dependent upon her portfolio performance, she can reallocate her remaining savings into vehicles that have greater growth potential (Playchecks). This means she can shift the remaining funds in her portfolio back to a 60/40 or 70/30 allocation and potentially receive higher returns on her investments.

Step 3: Incorporate Housing Wealth

Although Paula is comfortable with the initial amount of $40,000 per year, she knows that over time she will need to draw more annually because of inflation. This is where reverse mortgages can help.

Based on her age, home value ($375,000) and interest rate, the reverse mortgage made available a $141,625 line of credit growing around 5 percent. Paula has several ways she could incorporate the reverse mortgage line of credit (ReLOC) proceeds into her retirement plan.

(A) Paula can use the ReLOC as a growth bucket and take additional dollars in the years they are needed. In this way, the HECM acts as an inflation buffer.

(B) Paula can allow the ReLOC to continue growing. Down the road, as her needs change, she can turn on the monthly payment feature, which would be considerably larger at that time,

Age	LOC Amount	Tenure Pmt	5 Year Term	10 Year Term
65	$141,625	$769	$2,701	$1,539
70	$187,499	$1,074	$3,576	$2,037
75	$248,233	$1,536	$4,734	$2,697
80	$328,639	$2,273	$6,267	$3,570
85	$435,091	$3,567	$8,297	$4,727
90	$576,023	$6,258	$10,984	$6,258

and use it to supplement her needs. In this way, the HECM acts as an income buffer.

(C) Paula can also make use of the ReLOC bi-directionality feature. This means she can take money out when needed and put money back in to allow the line of credit to continue to grow.

This strategy gives Paula real flexibility. Her essential needs are covered with fixed income, her enjoyment needs are covered with a more aggressive investment allocation, and her inflation protection and any potential income needs are covered by the reverse mortgage.

It's hard to argue with the practical wisdom of the Paychecks/Playchecks and Buy Income/Invest the Difference strategies. It's even harder to improve upon them, but by combining guaranteed income, equity-based investments, and housing wealth, you can gain new options and tremendous peace of mind. (Not to mention that you look like a retirement savant.)

17

Long-Term Care Strategies for Protecting Assets and Legacy

I s it reasonable to think you may live a long life? If so, would it also be reasonable to expect that you could need some form of extended care (even for a short period of time)?

The truth is that most people will need care at some point in their lives, and while, of course, their lives are altered, the biggest impact will be the physical, emotional and financial costs to those they love.

As we consider long-term/extended in this chapter - both planning and paying for it - keep in mind it is an act of proactive thoughtfulness geared towards the ones we love most. That is our focus.

What Is Long-Term/Extended Care?

Long-term/extended care involves a variety of services designed to meet a person's health or personal care needs during a short or long period of time. These services help people live as independently and safely as possible when they can no longer perform everyday activities on their own i.e. bathing, dressing, toileting, eating, and moving around (like getting out of bed and into a chair).

When people hear the phrase "long-term care," they most often think of a nursing home, but according to the U.S. Department of Health and Human Services, more than 80% of long-term care is provided at home by unpaid family members and friends.

Care can also be given in a facility such as a nursing home, or in the community like an adult day care center, but the majority of those receiving long-term care are in their own homes.

People often need long-term care when they have a serious, ongoing health condition or disability. The need for long-term care can arise suddenly, such as after a heart attack or stroke, but most often, it develops gradually as people get older and more fragile, or as an illness or disability gets worse.

How Likely Am I to Need Extended Care?

The lifetime probability of becoming disabled in at least two activities of daily living, or of being cognitively impaired, is 68% for people age sixty-five and older.

How Much Does Extended Care Cost?

Recent studies show that the typical retiring couple can expect to spend at least $280,000 in out-of-pocket costs on health care plus an additional $130,000 for long-term/extended care.

While long-term care can be expensive, the cost goes beyond money. The emotional and physical toll on the family is steep.

Financially, cost differences are based on location, level of care, amenities, and level of privacy. The 2015 Genworth Cost of Care Survey explored the price of long-term care, breaking it down by category: nursing home (private vs. semi-private room), home health aide, homemaker services, assisted living facility and adult day health care.

For example, the national median cost per year of a private room in a nursing home was $91,250. However, in Alaska, that same service costs $281,415. By comparison, the same service in Oklahoma costs $60,225.

The numbers speak for themselves, and planning experts suggest that if you have assets or family to protect, establishing a long-term care plan is essential for your retirement.

Who Pays for Long-Term Care?

Some mistakenly believe that Medicare will cover long-term care costs. In some cases, Medicare does cover **up to 100 days** of rehabilitation in a qualified, skilled nursing facility, but not a day more.

MediCAID will cover long-term care costs for the impoverished. This safety net is a godsend for many, but in order to qualify, the recipient has to spend down most of their assets and give nearly all available income for care - oftentimes leaving very little for a remaining spouse. I know very few retirees willing to do this.

Living Arrangements for People Receiving Long-Term Care.

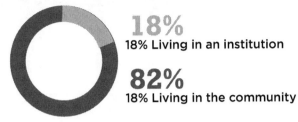

18%
18% Living in an institution

82%
18% Living in the community

All other retirees are responsible for their own long-term care plan. Often they will purchase long-term care insurance, or they may acquire a life insurance policy or annuity that has long-term care provisions built in.

Another option to consider is using your housing wealth. I've outlined seven strategies in the next section, and like any reverse mortgage strategy, they are designed for those who plan to remain in their homes for as long as possible.

7 Ways to Fund a Long-Term Care Plan with Housing Wealth

Self-Inure - HECM Line of Credit Strategy

Establish a growing reserve of dollars with a HECM Line of Credit and use those funds as needed to cover long-term care costs without having the burden of a mandatory monthly loan payment. This strategy works best when the line of credit is established at the onset of retirement. (Chapter 7)

Maximize Your "Self-Insure Fund" - HECM Exchange Strategy

If you're financially comfortable making monthly loan payments, continue doing so, but on the reverse mortgage. This reduces the outstanding balance of the HECM, while simultaneously adding funds to the available and growing line of credit for tax-free access in the future. (Chapter 10)

Premium Replacement – HECM Monthly Payment Strategy

If premium payments are a burden on your monthly budget, convert your HECM Line of Credit to monthly payments and use the funds to cover your daily living expenses. (Chapter 8)

Age	LOC Amount	Tenure Pmt	5 Year Term	10 Year Term
65	$141,625	$769	$2,701	$1,539
70	$187,499	$1,074	$3,576	$2,037
75	$248,233	$1,536	$4,734	$2,697
80	$328,639	$2,273	$6,267	$3,570
85	$435,091	$3,567	$8,297	$4,727
90	$576,023	$6,258	$10,984	$6,258

Don't forget that proceeds from a reverse mortgage should not be used to purchase or make direct payments on a product (like long-term insurance). In this case, the premium payments are coming from your income/savings, while the reverse mortgage covers your daily essentials.

Premium Replacement - HECM Replacement Strategy

Use the HECM Replacement strategy to pay off your housing related loan. Now the money that was going towards your loan payment each month can be reallocated to cover long-term care insurance premiums. (Chapter 9)

Acquire Insurance - HECM for Purchase Strategy

Having proceeds left over after selling a home is normal for any retiree. Using the HECM for purchase program is no different as it also will often result in remaining proceeds after the sale of the departure home. You can look to those proceeds to strengthen your long-term care plan with extended care insurance coverage of some kind. (Chapter 11)

Gap Funding – HECM Monthly Payment Strategy

While your long-term care or life insurance should cover much of your cost, it may not cover everything. HECM monthly payments can help bridge the gap between what your insurance covers and what it does not. It can also fill in if you must leave your job early and need funding until your policy kicks in. (Chapter 8)

Policy Pricing - HECM Line of Credit Strategy

For those who can qualify for and afford it, traditional long-term care insurance may be the best way to cover long-term care costs. However, to some, this type of insurance is considered more expensive. There are four pricing features on these policies, that when adjusted, can make the price more affordable.

- √ **Benefit Amount:** How much per day your policy will pay
- √ **Benefit Period:** How long that amount will be paid for
- √ **Inflation Protection:** How your benefit amount keeps pace with inflation over time
- √ **Waiting Period:** How long will it take before the policy begins paying

Any adjustment in these four features can have a significant impact on premium costs. This is where the reverse mortgage can help. Not only can the repurposed mortgage payments cover the premium, but the establishing of the line of credit can create additional options.

For example, you could choose a lower benefit amount or a shorter benefit period because the HECM line of credit can be converted to monthly payments to cover the shortfall.

You could also use the HECM line of credit growth as an inflation rider - allowing the inflation rider on the other policy to be lowered or even eliminated.

Finally, you could extend the waiting period; the longer the waiting period, the lower the premium for the policy. If you have medical expenses during the prolonged waiting period, pull from your established HECM line of credit to fund them.

Can you see how Housing Wealth gives you the flexibility to structure your policy and premium payments in a way that substantially reduces coverage costs?

Protecting your health (and your assets) is an important feature of your retirement plan. Incorporating Housing Wealth can give you some options that might otherwise not have been available to you. This is also true when it comes to taxes in retirement, as you'll see in the next chapter.

18

Creating a Tax-Free Retirement with Roth Conversions

Remember the Mount Everest illustration from earlier in the book? On the way up the mountain (accumulation period), the goal is acquiring money and ensuring your assets are allocated to maximize growth and minimizing risk.

As you begin retirement and head down the mountain (distribution phase), a different focus emerges - drawing income from the assets you've acquired. But where should you draw money from first? Traditionally, retirees have had three retirement income sources from which to choose:

√ **Taxable:** CDs, Brokerage Accounts, etc.

√ **Tax Deferred:** Traditional IRA, 401(k) or 403(b), Annuities, etc.

√ **Tax-Free:** Roth IRAs

According to the Retirement Income Certified Professionals (RICP®) program at the American College, retirees should first withdraw money from their taxable accounts - allowing their traditional IRAs and other tax-deferred accounts to compound for as long as possible.

The Role of Tax-Free Dollars in Retirement

The last source from which to draw income is tax-free investments like the Roth IRA. Retirement Income planners give special emphasis to Roths because their growth is not taxable; they have no minimum required distributions; and they carry specific legacy planning benefits. You may have already read about the benefits of converting a traditional IRA to a Roth IRA for the same reasons I just mentioned.

IRA expert, PBS show host, and CPA, Ed Slott was recently asked: what are the benefits of a Roth IRA?

"First, the idea of a Roth conversion is, you are moving money from a taxable IRA or even a 401(k) to a tax-free Roth, and there's a cost to that. You pay tax on the taxable amount converted. It adds to your income.

But the benefit is, once it's in a Roth IRA in retirement, once you have five years and 59 1/2 years old, that money grows tax-free forever. Remember, tax-free money always grows the fastest because it's not eroded by current or future taxes.

The most important element, seldom mentioned, is that there are no required minimum distributions at 70 with Roth IRAs like you have for IRAs. Now, lots of people with IRAs don't like being forced to take distributions at 70 1/2, but with a Roth IRA, you're not forced to take out money you don't need, which saves you from paying a higher tax bill."

Calvin and Claire's Roth Conversion

Let's take a look at what a Roth Conversion did for one couple's retirement.

Client Overview: Calvin and Claire (65) are fairly comfortable with their retirement income plan, but they are somewhat concerned about living longer than they've planned for. They're fearful of the impact future tax rates may have on their savings, should they need to use them, or on their estate should they pass it on.

Financial Position:

- $200,000 Traditional IRA | $400,000 401k/Annuities |
- $100,000 in Brokerage Account
- $450,000 Home | $50,000 Mortgage | $541/m Payment

Planning Objective: Convert the tax-deferred IRA into a tax-free Roth IRA for future use, or as an inheritance, while preserving the most amount of principal possible.

The Roth Conversion Conversation

Calvin and Claire called their accountant who began the Roth Conversion conversation by exploring three questions:

1. Do you need the money in your traditional IRA immediately or in the future? They won't need it until later in retirement, so they proceed.

2. Are you concerned that you may be in a higher tax bracket in the future? Yes, that is one of their concerns, especially in the midst of today's economic uncertainty.

3. Do you have the money to pay the taxes on the conversion? Yes, they think so but they're not sure the best assets to use.

There Is a Third Option

Three Options for Paying the Conversion Taxes

Let's say the taxes to roll over their $200,000 traditional IRA into a Roth IRA will be $48,000. Calvin and Claire's accountant lays out a few choices regarding the accounts they could draw from.

√   They could pay the taxes out of the rollover itself. Instead of rolling over $200,000, they roll over $152,000. However, then they don't receive the full benefit of the transaction.

√   They could take the $48,000 from their existing IRA or other taxable account. Doing so would mean paying taxes on the IRA distribution as well as incurring the lost opportunity costs from drawing the money early instead of allowing it to continue compounding.

Herein lies the challenge; many people don't have a viable source to pay the conversion taxes, or they need the funds to live on. Simply stated: if you don't have money to pay the taxes, you can't convert.

Use Your Housing Wealth

We know that the majority of older Americans and emerging baby boomers are sitting on a source for paying Roth Conversion taxes: their homes! How can Housing Wealth be used to pay the taxes for a Roth IRA conversion? The process is easier than you may think.

First, Calvin and Claire calculate their HECM benefit. After paying off the $50,000 mortgage on their $450,000 home, the HECM makes a $118,000 line of credit available.

Line of Credit Left Untouched

Age	Beginning of Year Balance	Growth (%5)	End of Year Balance
65	$118,000.00	$5,900.00	$123,900.00
70	$150,601.22	$7,530.06	$158,131.29
75	$192,209.57	$9,610.48	$201,820.04
80	$245,313.53	$12,265.68	$257,579.20
85	$313,089.13	$15,654.46	$328,743.59
90	$399,589.88	$19,979.49	$419,569.38

Next, they determine if they want to pay the taxes all at once or over a period of time (let's say, for example, a 5 or 10-year period). If they decide to pay the conversion taxes over 5 years, they divide the $48,000 by 5 and see they must pull $9,600 each year from the HECM line of credit. If over 10 years, the amount would be $4,800 per year.

Look at the three illustrations to see how the line of credit fares. Pay close attention to the remaining (and growing) balance in the latter years of their retirement.

Line of Credit Growth with One-Time Tax Payment of $48,000 in 1st Year

Age	Beginning of Year Balance	Growth (%5)	Withdrawal	End of Year Balance
65	$118,000.00	$5,900.00	$48,000.00	$75,900.00
70	$92,256.92	$4,612.85	$0	$96,869.77
75	$117,745.81	$5,887.29	$0	$123,633.10
80	$150,276.81	$7,513.84	$0	$157,790.65
85	$191,795.52	$9,589.78	$0	$201,385.30
90	$244,785.09	$12,239.25	$0	$257,024.34

Line of Credit Growth with Taxes Paid
Over 5-Year Period

Age	Beginning of Year Balance	Growth (%5)	Withdrawal	End of Year Balance
65	$118,000.00	$5,900.00	$9,600.00	$114,300.00
66	$114,300.00	$5,715.00	$9,600.00	$110,415.00
67	$110,415.00	$5,520.75	$9,600.00	$106,335.75
68	$106,335.75	$5,316.79	$9,600.00	$102,052.54
69	$102,052.54	$5,102.63	$9,600.00	$97,555.16
70	$97,555.16	$4,877.76	$0	$102,432.92
75	$124,507.86	$6,225.39	$0	$130,733.25
80	$158,907.08	$7,945.35	$0	$166,852.44
85	$202,810.18	$10,140.51	$0	$212,950.69
90	$258,842.89	$12,942.14	$0	$271,785.04

Line of Credit Growth with Taxes Paid
Over 10-Year Period

Age	Beginning of Year Balance	Growth (%5)	Withdrawal	End of Year Balance
65	$118,000.00	$5,900.00	$4,800.00	$119,100.00
66	$119,100.00	$5,955.00	$4,800.00	$120,255.00
67	$120,255.00	$6,012.75	$4,800.00	$121,467.75
68	$121,467.75	$6,073.39	$4,800.00	$122,741.14
69	$122,741.14	$6,137.06	$4,800.00	$124,078.19
70	$124,078.19	$6,203.91	$4,800.00	$125,482.10
71	$125,482.10	$6,274.11	$4,800.00	$126,956.21
72	$126,956.21	$6,347.81	$4,800.00	$128,504.02
73	$128,504.02	$6,425.20	$4,800.00	$130,129.22
74	$130,129.22	$6,506.46	$4,800.00	$131,835.68
75	$131,835.68	$6,591.78	$0	$138,427.47
80	$168,259.45	$8,412.97	$0	$176,672.42
85	$214,746.43	$10,737.32	$0	$225,483.76
90	$274,076.91	$13,703.85	$0	$287,780.76

Notice that in each of the scenarios, Calvin and Claire have funds remaining in their HECM Line of Credit. If they choose to do the conversion over a longer period of time, they will have more in the line of credit because they have taken advantage of its growth factor.

By using the HECM to pay all (or some) of the taxes for the conversion they were able to:

√ Convert the entire $200,000 into tax-free savings for their retirement needs, or for their heirs.

√ Have continued access to HECM Line of Credit even AFTER the conversion.

You may have considered a Roth Conversion strategy in the past, but not been able to pay the taxes in a way that made financial sense. Now, you have another option to consider - Housing Wealth.

19

Seven Housing Wealth Strategies that Benefit Women

The financial and retirement planning concerns of women are very different from those of men. A cursory internet search will reveal that:

- Women are less likely to have planned or saved enough for retirement (primarily because they spent fewer years in the workforce, made less when they did and often left early to take care of a family member).

- For women age 65+, the poverty rate is nearly double that of men in the same age group.

- 27% of gray divorced women are poor compared to just 11% of gray divorced men.

- Women are far more likely to report that their financial concerns are causing them stress.

- Only one-third of women believe they are on track for retirement planning and saving.

On top of that, recent studies say that 90% of women will be the sole financial decision maker at some point in their life!

As we close out our advanced strategies section, I want to bring to your attention to a few HECM strategies that, I believe, have greater relevance for women than men. The first few I will simply highlight, since they have already been covered, and I will expand upon the last one: Gray Divorce.

1. Paying Off a Mortgage

Nothing is more concerning to retirees than carrying debt into their retirement years. The sad fact is that consumer and housing debt will eat up a very large portion of the modern retiree's monthly income and peace of mind.

This concern is magnified for the married woman due to the near-certain income reduction that she will experience at the death of her spouse. Having the HECM Replacement or Exchange conversation is a way to alleviate some of her future concerns. (Chapter 9 & 10)

2. Creating an Income Replacement Strategy

Similarly, because the income for most women will be adjusted at the death of their spouse, an established HECM can often supplement needed income.

To optimize the amount of income the HECM could replace, a wise strategy may be to establish it as a line of credit early in retirement and let it grow as a type of income replacement insurance. It can be accessed and replaced as needed or converted to monthly income if the loan is still in force.

Having this conversation early can ease the mind of wives as well as single women who desire a buffer asset to hedge against market volatility.

Additionally, many pension systems are hurting and in danger of collapse. At the very least, they are being restructured, so that employees must now pay for medical expenses. A recent Forbes article said nearly one million U.S. workers and retirees are currently covered by pension plans on the verge of collapse. Establishing a standby HECM line of credit could serve as a much-needed lifeline. (Chapters 7 & 8)

3. Creating a Long-Term Care Plan

In an earlier chapter, I mentioned that nearly 70 percent of Americans will need some sort of long-term care during their lifetimes with the average length being nearly three years.

Thirty percent of the primary caregivers are over the age of sixty-five. Oftentimes, both the literal and figurative heavy lifting of caregiving falls on the wife, and it is typically she who will suffer the indignity of having someone else care for her. This is a gloomy, often overlooked reality that weighs heavily on females.

Using housing wealth to help create a long-term care plan is very wise; having a plan is better than having none, especially for women! (Chapter 17)

4. Life Insurance

A very simple way to help the longer-living spouse is to establish or maintain life insurance that can fulfill a variety of functions upon the death of the first spouse as well as legacy benefits at the passing of the second. For pennies on the dollar, retirees can establish a policy or set up a reserve fund to ensure there is enough to finance the rest of retirement. (Chapter 9)

5. Right Size with HECM for Purchase

Even though the house may become too large and expenses burdensome, the value of homeownership is still important to many retirees. However, the burden of homeownership is often exacerbated in mid to late retirement when funds are tight or perhaps a sickness or death drains income and savings. Using the HECM for Purchase allows retirees to purchase their next home for around 50 to 60 percent down, have no monthly mortgage payments and often add new dollars back into savings. For wives/widows and caregivers, this could be a real blessing. (Chapter 11)

6. Social Security and Retirement Income Optimization

One of the most significant ways to optimize retirement outcomes is to have a very simple conversation regarding Social Security. You can defer taking Social Security by establishing a HECM line of credit at the onset of retirement and then drawing from it to supplement all or a portion of what you are waiting for Social Security to provide.

7. Gray Divorce, Silver Solutions

In an article entitled, "Gray Divorce Boosts Poverty Level for Women," financial author, Mary Beth Franklin, shares about the growing phenomenon of gray divorce and how women are particularly impacted by it. Here are a few excerpts:

√ Even though the overall U.S. divorce rate has remained stable since 1990, gray divorce has doubled during that period.

√ Gray divorce appears to diminish wealth more than earlier divorce, and women are impacted in a greater measure than men are.

√ Gender matters and economic disparity between men and women widens with age. A whopping 27 percent of gray divorced women are low-income, compared to just 11 percent of gray divorced men.

Divorce is always painful, but if there is a home involved, there may be some solutions that create a real win/win, especially for women.

Four Options for Betty and John to Equitably Divide the Assets

 Option 1: Sell and Go Their Separate Ways

The home is sold for $400,000 and the proceeds divided. Betty and John each get $200,000 to go and start over. The possibilities? A rental situation, a smaller home, or a larger home with a monthly mortgage payment.

 Option 2: Buy Out with Traditional Refinance

Betty decides to buy John out. She obtains a traditional mortgage refinance for $200,000 and gives that cash to John. Betty keeps the house and now has a monthly mortgage payment for the next twenty to thirty years.

 Option 3: Take Out a HECM and Stay

Betty gets a reverse mortgage on the existing home. The HECM makes available around $200,000. Betty gives that money to her ex-husband. Now she can stay in the home without any mortgage payments required.

 Option 4: HECM for Purchase

The home is sold, and Betty takes her $200,000 payout. She wants to purchase a home for $300,000 but she does not want to have a traditional mortgage with monthly payments. She also does not want to pull $100,000 from her savings.

Betty's son told her she can use the HECM for Purchase program to move into the $300,000 home for around $156,000 down, have no monthly mortgage payments, preserve her savings, and still have $44,000 left over from her divorce settlement.

The following chart shows she could also move into a $375,000 home or $200,000 home and still add new dollars to her savings.

Proceeds from Sale	New Home Price	HECM Proceeds	Down Payment	Liberated Proceeds
$200,000	$300,000	$144,000	$156,000	$44,000
$200,000	$375,000	$180,000	$195,000	$5,000
$200,000	$200,000	$96,000	$104,000	$96,000

Divorce is never pleasant but it can be especially problematic for women. Implementing the HECM for Purchase (when coordinated with other assets) can be a real life-changer.

A Final Word

Congratulations again! You have completed the Advanced Strategies section for the reverse mortgage. You now understand ways to use housing wealth to mitigate market risk and volatility, enhance a fixed income strategy, prepare for long-term care, create tax diversification with a Roth IRA, and better equip women for retirement. That's a lot of valuable information.

In the end, it wasn't really that hard, was it? Most people want to have an enjoyable retirement without stress and worry, and most retirees own a home. When we combine those two factors in a planning conversation, the outcomes can, as you have seen, make all the difference in the world.

Online Resources at a Glance

- www.HousingWealthCalculator.com
- www.HousingWealthVideos.com
- www.HousingWealthPartners.com
- www.HousingWealth.net

For more information, or to contact the author, go to www.HousingWealth.net or email AskDonGraves@gmail.com

Appendix: 25 Ways to Use a Reverse Mortgage

☐ Pay off your forward mortgage to reduce your monthly expenses.

☐ Remodel your home to accommodate aging limitations.

☐ Maintain a line of credit (that grows) for health emergencies and surprises.

☐ Cover monthly expenses and hold on to other assets while their value continues to grow.

☐ Cover monthly expenses and avoid selling assets at depressed values.

☐ Pay for health insurance during early retirement years until Medicare eligible at 65.

☐ Pay your Medicare Part B and Part D costs.

☐ Combine life tenure payments with Social Security and income generated by assets to replace your salary and maintain your monthly routine of paying bills from new income.

☐ Pay for your children's or grandchildren's college or professional education.

☐ Maintain a "standby" cash reserve to get you through the ups and downs of investment markets and give you more flexibility.

☐ Combine proceeds with the sale of one home to buy a new home without a forward mortgage and monthly mortgage payments.

☐ Pay for long-term care needs.

☐ Fill the gap in a retirement plan caused by lower than expected returns on your assets.

☐ Pay for short-term, in-home care, or physical therapy following an accident or medical episode.

- ☐ Pay for a retirement plan, estate plan, or a will.

- ☐ Convert a room or basement to a living facility for an aging parent, relative, or caregiver.

- ☐ Set up transportation arrangements for when you are no longer comfortable driving.

- ☐ Create a set aside to pay real estate taxes and property insurance.

- ☐ Delay collecting Social Security benefit until it maxes out at age 70.

- ☐ Eliminate credit card debt and avoid building new credit debt.

- ☐ Cover monthly expenses in between jobs or during career transition without utilizing other saved assets.

- ☐ Cover expenses and avoid capital gains tax consequences of selling off other assets.

- ☐ Purchase health-related technology that enables you to live in-home alone.

- ☐ Pay for an Uber or Lyft account so you have mobility and access to appointments and social activities.

- ☐ Help your adult children through family emergencies.

ABOUT DON GRAVES

Don Graves, RICP®, CLTC®, CSA, is one of the nation's leading educators on HECM reverse mortgages in retirement income planning. He is the president and founder of the HECM Institute for Housing Wealth Studies and is an adjunct professor of retirement income at The American College of Financial Services. He was the first reverse mortgage professional to obtain the coveted Retirement Income Certified Professional (RICP®) designation from The American College and was recently recognized as one of the top eleven retirement income alumni to read.

Don has a knack for common-sense analysis and application, a strategic focus on advanced reverse mortgage education, and nearly two decades of experience in the home equity retirement planning space. His course at The American College currently has more than 16,000 advisors enrolled, and his personal practice has generated more than 12,000 HECM consultations, leading to nearly 3,000 clients over the last twenty years.

As both an educator and skilled practitioner, Don has a unique perspective that very few share. His Retirement Income Certified Professional (RICP®) designation equips him to utilize the powerful principles and strategies regarding retirement income planning: its design, intent, risks, and limitations. Furthermore, as a reverse mortgage professional, he understands the unique needs and concerns that consumers have, along with their hesitation when it comes to reverse mortgages. He is masterful in showing how and where housing wealth and reverse mortgages intersect with retirement income planning.

Don has been quoted in *Forbes* magazine and featured on PBS-sponsored shows as well as other venues and programming. He is a sought-after professional speaker when it comes to the changing face of reverse mortgages and how they can seamlessly incorporate with comprehensive retirement income plans.

He holds an undergraduate degree in finance from Temple University, as well as graduate studies in economics at Eastern University. Don resides in Greater Philadelphia, is married, and has three children and one grandchild.

www.HousingWealth.net

Made in the USA
Middletown, DE
18 June 2020